RICHER THAN A MILLIONAIRE

ONE
MAN'S
JOURNEY
TO GOD

PAUL WALDMANN

LIGUORI
PUBLICATIONS

ONE LIGUORI DRIVE
LIGUORI, MISSOURI 63057-9999
(314) 464-2500

To Adonai,
Who never ceased to smile at me.

☆ ☆ ☆

ISBN 0-89243-414-7
Library of Congress Catalog Card Number: 91-76661

Copyright © 1992, Paul Waldmann
Printed in U.S.A.

Cover design by Chris Sharp

CONTENTS

Childhood

Adolescence

Young Adulthood

Hitler

Journey to America

My New Country

Discerning the Will of God

The Infinite

CHILDHOOD

1910-1916
WHY DID THE LITTLE
BOY HATE ME?

I was born in Vienna, Austria. The year was 1910, and the day — I hesitate to tell you — was the first of April. My parents named me Kurt; I changed my name to Paul many years later. What was the Vienna of my childhood like? It was a charming city. I remember the magnificent parks with their bandstands and outdoor cafés, and of course, the enchanting Vienna woods that surround the city with their gently rolling hills and sunlit meadows — a paradise on earth. I had no brothers or sisters, and there were no small children where we lived, so I had to provide my own entertainment. I busied myself with building blocks and paper and pencil. By the time I was five, I could read and write.

One day I got tired of it all and decided on a life of crime. I found a cane, took it into the corridor, and whacked everyone

5

who came up the stairs. Most people just smiled and patted me on the head. But one lady gave me a slap on the face. I began to bawl and ran home.

That taught me a great lesson. It even inspired me to write a little poem. It was about two boys: one very bad, the other very good. The bad boy was nothing but trouble, while everybody loved the good boy. Such was my newfound philosophy, but I soon found out "it ain't necessarily so." One morning on my way to school — I had just started first grade — out of a doorway stepped a boy who blocked my way. Before I could ask him why he had stopped me, he spat in my face and said, "There! Dirty Jew!"

I was more confused than hurt. I didn't know who the boy was or why he spat at me. And I didn't know what he meant by "dirty Jew."

1916-1921
A JEW BY
ANY OTHER NAME

*A*t school there was a crucifix above the blackboard (Austria was a Catholic country), and every morning the Catholics stood and recited some prayers, while we Jews just stood there. I didn't know what the prayers were, nor had I ever seen a crucifix before. But it didn't faze me; to me it was just part of being in school.

Once a week a priest came to teach the Catholics their religion, and we Jews had to go to a different classroom where a rabbi taught us Hebrew prayers. Each month the Catholics marched in double file to the nearby church for something they called confession, while we just went home. There was still one other distinction: We stayed home on Jewish holidays, but the Catholics had to go to school. I didn't know what it all meant; I just knew that we were different from them: We were Jews. When I got my first report card, I became confused. It read, Name: Kurt Waldmann. Religion: Mosaic. "Mosaic? What's that?" My mother said, "That's the same as Jewish." She didn't elaborate. Only many years later did I understand:

Refined people referred to us as "Israelites," and our religion — since it had come down through Moses — was called "Mosaic." *Jew* was a dirty word.

☆ ☆ ☆

At school I made friends with a Jewish boy whose name was Eugene. We took to each other instinctively, starting a friendship which lasted into our teens, and even beyond.

School hours were from eight to twelve; since homework was minimal, Eugene and I had afternoons and weekends free. Soon Eugene's home became my second home. His mother was an excellent cook, and I had a standing invitation to eat with them. She often said to me lovingly, "Kurt is my second son."

Eugene and I discovered we had a mutual love for the theater. Together we read the dramas of Ibsen, Schiller, and Goethe. Soon we began to write our own dramas. They were full of long-winded monologues, and in each one some nobleman gave his life "for the glory of the king."

Eugene and I not only wrote the dramas, we also acted them. He and I played all the parts. Many of our dramas ended with a procession. We slowly and solemnly walked around the dining-room table in the direction of the stove, which represented the guillotine, and there I had my head chopped off "for the glory of the king." Then the imaginary curtain on our imaginary stage fell, and Eugene and I looked at each other smilingly and congratulated each other on the completion of another masterpiece.

☆ ☆ ☆

But don't think that writing plays was all we ever did. Eugene and I — and Eugene's father — were avid soccer fans. We went to games Sunday after Sunday, summer and winter, rain or snow. Very often I caught cold standing in the wet snow, but the following Sunday, despite my mother's pleading, I went to the game again — and caught cold again.

☆ ☆ ☆

Every Friday afternoon, Eugene's mother placed two candlesticks on the dining-room table, and at sunset she placed a kerchief on her head, lighted the candles, covered her eyes with her hands, and silently said the Sabbath prayer. I had never seen anything like it at our house. My parents did not observe any of the laws or customs of the Jewish religion. Yet my mother had strong faith in God; I often heard her thank God for small things, such as an exceptionally delicious meal or a pleasant day in the country. When troubles came — and she had an overabundance of them — she never lost her sparkling sense of humor. With a smile she quietly said, "God will help." My father, on the other hand, showed no interest in anything connected with religion.

☆ ☆ ☆

Each Friday evening, Eugene and his parents went to the synagogue for Sabbath services, and they often invited me to come along. I always felt self-conscious. I didn't know the Hebrew prayers these people were saying, and I thought everybody was looking at the boy who didn't pray. I was always glad when services were over; yet at the same time, I looked forward to coming back on the next Friday.

☆ ☆ ☆

I had eleven cousins on my father's side and six on my mother's; but the one I saw most often was my cousin Hans. He was — and still is — different from anyone I ever knew. He and I were extreme opposites; that's what attracted me to him.

Hans, a handsome boy with dark, mysterious eyes, was a year younger than I. He fascinated me. Always full of ideas

9

for unusual things to do, his favorite expression was "I'll tell you what we'll do." We took long walks through the streets and parks of Vienna, during which he eagerly whispered into my ear all his plans about the things we could *do*.

It was this same Hans who befriended me later in life when I needed help most: first in Vienna and again on the day I arrived in the United States. (But I'm getting ahead of my story.)

☆ ☆ ☆

When I was nine years old, my mother and I spent the entire summer in the country. She knew a Jewish family who owned a house there, and they had invited us to visit. They had a son my age, a tall, slim boy with the appearance of a young Austrian aristocrat. His name was Franz. There was a beautiful, large garden outside Franz's house, and he and I had a glorious time playing all the games two nine-year-olds could think up. One day we played circus, and the next day we were a fire department. And then we decided to play school. For a week we took turns being teacher and pupil. Some of the neighbors got wind of it and wanted to send us their children for private lessons. That's when we went back to being a circus. The summer was sheer delight — until one day....

I had talked Franz into putting on a play with me, although he had no interest in acting. But I was a born ham. We selected a corner in the garden to be our stage, and there we began our play. I was just in the midst of an ad-libbed monologue when I heard shouting. I turned around and saw some boys at the top of the garden wall grinning and mimicking my way of speaking. Then they began to yell in unison, "Hey, hey! Get the Jews! Hey, hey! Get the Jews!"

Franz and I ran into the house to hide our embarrassment, the sarcastic laughter of the boys ringing in our ears.

☆ ☆ ☆

When I was eleven, I graduated from elementary school. *No, I was not a genius.* Elementary school in Austria had only five grades, and everybody, except outright nincompoops, graduated at age eleven. I was now ready for secondary school.

1921-1923
LITTLE MONEY —
LITTLE EDUCATION

*I*f you were an eleven-year-old in Vienna, you could choose from a variety of secondary schools. The choice would depend on your aptitude, your plans for the future, and your parents' financial circumstances. There were private schools that could prepare you for entrance into the university, and schools for those who aspired to a career in finance or business. The entire curriculum in any of these schools required six or seven years of study. And tuition differed from school to school.

But there was one other choice: the public school. It took only three years to complete — and it was free. In our family, money was always in short supply. So, to the public school I went.

☆ ☆ ☆

No longer could I spend whole afternoons and weekends with my friend Eugene. He had entered one of the private schools and had far more homework than I. All at once I had time on my hands. I looked into the extracurricular subjects taught at my school and decided on French.

Our teacher was a native Parisian: a tall, well-dressed man. His teaching method was unique. He brought French newspapers to class and had us read them, though we barely understood what we read. He insisted that the first thing to learn was pronunciation; everything else could follow later.

After a year I could pronounce French with the best, but I still could not speak it, except for simple sentences like "I open the window. I close the door." Hardly enough for a conversation. So I quit French and decided to try English.

I loved English right from the start; it seemed almost a second language to me. In no time at all, I had learned about a thousand English words, had written them in a little notebook, and was able to rattle them off forward and backward.

I soon realized there was a problem with "forward and backward." I had to know any word at any time *instantly*. I had to get the words out of that book and into my head. But how?

One day it came to me: I took large sheets of paper and cut them into small squares. On each of these squares, I wrote an English word, and on the back I wrote the German translation. I put all these little pieces of paper into an old cigar box, closed the lid, shook the box, and held a drawing. If I drew a German word, I had to know its English translation *instantly,* and vice versa. I held this lottery every day for about an hour. As I learned new words, they also went into the cigar box. Thus I acquired what I considered a good knowledge of English.

Then one day came my opportunity to put all that learning to use, but I failed the test. It was a beautiful day so I took a walk through Vienna's elegant downtown, past the opera, along the Kaerntnerstrasse with its exclusive shops. I gazed at the store windows and daydreamed of being rich so I could buy all those luxurious items. Suddenly, a stocky woman in a gray-tweed suit stopped me along the way. With the bark of a drill sergeant, she asked, "Speak English?" I was so intimidated, I forgot all about the cigar box and the little pieces of paper. I could only stammer, "No." She turned abruptly and walked away.

☆ ☆ ☆

My friend Eugene was the last person I would have expected to invite me to see a movie about Jesus. Yet one afternoon he wanted to know if I would like to go to a show. I asked what was playing. He said it was called "Passion Play." I had no idea what that was, but I went along.

It was very confusing. I didn't understand any of it. There were a lot of people talking excitedly and running around with torches. Then they arrested Jesus and killed him.

On the way home, Eugene said, "This Jesus must have been a Jew, since that was the only religion at his time." I had never given it any thought, but Eugene was probably right. This Jesus must have been a Jew.

I wondered why they killed him. Eugene had the answer to that. "Because he was a Jew and wanted to start his own religion."

☆ ☆ ☆

The rabbi at school came one day and reminded me that soon I would be thirteen years old and should begin preparation for my bar mitzvah. (A word to the uninformed; and *no one* was more uninformed than I: Bar mitzvah is a solemn moment in the life of a Jewish boy, the moment when he becomes an adult member of the religious community.)

The rabbi gave me some Hebrew prayers to study, my mother bought me a new suit for the occasion, and one Saturday morning my parents and I walked to the nearby synagogue.

It was a large, impressive building. Seated toward the front, I saw another boy and his parents. We also sat down and waited. I was filled with a sense of joyous anticipation. After a few minutes, an elderly rabbi appeared, ascended a platform, and called my name. I went up to him, he pointed at a large book, and from it I read the Hebrew prayer I had studied. When I finished, he asked me to return to my seat; then he called the other boy. Just as the boy began to read, my father said, "That's all. Let's go." And we left immediately.

Near the door, I turned around and saw the rabbi giving us a questioning look. I realized then that the ceremony had just barely begun and that we were walking out on my bar mitzvah. I felt very ashamed.

Outside, my father lit one of his stogies, and we went home. There was no joy in my heart — only emptiness.

1923-1924

A STAR FOR A DAY

*S*omething unbelievable happened one morning during the school year of 1923. The principal came to our classroom and asked me to come with him. All eyes were on us as we left the room.

He explained that they were planning a big celebration for the school's fiftieth anniversary. They had rented one of the largest theaters in Vienna for a gala performance to be given by students exclusively — and I had been chosen to be one of the performers.

I walked back to the classroom in a daze. *I would perform at a theater!* It was a ham's fondest dream come true.

I was given two poems to memorize, and one of the teachers rehearsed them with me.

Then the great day came. I put on the new suit my mother had bought me for my bar mitzvah, and my parents and I went to the theater.

The place was enormous, and it was filled to capacity — perhaps a thousand people were there. I looked at the large stage and realized that soon I would be there — all alone, facing all those people — and my throat tightened.

Backstage the young performers stood in a corner, their faces showing varying degrees of stage fright. The houselights dimmed and the bright stage lights came on as the principal walked on stage to greet the audience, and the show started.

I was number four on the program, and I could hardly wait until my turn would come; then I'd have the ordeal behind me. I was numb with stage fright.

Just then I heard the principal say to my teacher, "Let Waldmann be last; he is the best."

Cold panic hit me. My stomach suddenly felt as if it had a hole in it. I am the best? What if I lost my voice? What if I forgot my lines? What if… I don't know how I lived the next hour until I heard my name announced.

With shaking knees, I walked on stage. I looked at the faces in the audience — and at that moment something happened to me. *I lost my fear.* Suddenly, I felt nothing but the determination to excel.

I began to recite the first poem. It was a dramatic piece, and I poured every ounce of my energy and the very depths of my emotions into it. There was absolute silence in the audience — not a whisper. When I finished, there was a storm of applause. It filled the large theater and warmed my boyish heart.

I followed up with the second poem: a short, comical piece. Again there was long applause. I smiled my thank-you, bowed, and walked off the stage. My panic had turned into joy. The near disaster I dreaded so much had become a triumph.

☆ ☆ ☆

A year passed. I was fourteen now and in my last semester of school. One of our teachers kept telling us how different our lives would be from that time on, that soon we would be facing the "real world." I had no idea what this real world was. Then one day they handed me my report card, and I walked out of school for the last time.

A few days later I happened to meet the principal on the street. He asked if I had any plans for more schooling. "You were always a good student," he said. "Perhaps a business school or a…" I interrupted, "We have no money for that. I have to get a job."

He shook his head in disappointment. As he walked away, I heard him say, "It's a pity…."

ADOLESCENCE

SEPTEMBER 1924

A BEAST OF BURDEN

*M*y first employment — at a gloomy little place on a dreary side street — lasted exactly two weeks. I was hired as an apprentice to a leather wholesaler.

At first, my mother was very happy. She had heard of a man who had started a leather business on a shoestring and had become quite wealthy. She thought if I could learn the business, perhaps I too…

However, it didn't look like I would *learn* anything, simply because nobody bothered to *teach* me anything. The owner never spoke to me, and the three employees didn't say much either, except when they wanted me to make a delivery. I — a skinny fourteen-year-old, lugged heavy bundles by streetcar all across the city.

Then came the day when they hung on my shoulder a load that nearly broke my back. It was a long, thick roll of black leather. The enormous weight of it forced me to walk bent down, and I could barely see where I was going. With every step the thick roll hit against my ankles and almost tripped me.

They handed me the fare for the streetcar, a slip of paper with the customer's address, and sent me on my way. One hour later, I climbed off the streetcar; since I could not look up, I ran head-on into a man.

I apologized, but he quickly reassured me. In his voice was such kindness, such unusual warmth, that I forced myself to raise my head and look at him.

I didn't believe my eyes! HE WAS A PRIEST! I didn't know what to say or do. I just wanted to get away from him. I had never known any priests or nuns, and *I didn't want to know any*. They gave me the creeps. I mumbled something, turned around, and shuffled off. The whole thing seemed like a nightmare: first the humiliation of having to carry this load and now this priest!

I found the customer's place, got rid of my burden, and went straight home — never to return to the leather dealer.

1924-1928

STUMBLING INTO

ADULTHOOD

I found another job very soon; actually, my uncle, a promi-
nent man in Vienna's business circle, found it for me.

At this place, I felt at home. The three owners were pleasant
and considerate, and my immediate boss was a true gentleman
who taught me many valuable skills. Their firm — one of
Vienna's foremost — manufactured men's clothing. I spent
four and a half happy years there.

However, one of the workers proved to be a very irritating
fellow apprentice named Ernest. He was a schemer. Because
he sometimes succeeded in pulling the wool over my eyes, he
became a bit overblown with conceit. I often caught him looking
at me with a disdainful and sarcastic grin. Oddly enough, it was
this grin that — some years later — saved my life.

☆ ☆ ☆

The twenties were the years when all of Vienna flocked to
see the great operettas by Lehár and Strauss, the world-famous
Die Fledermaus, The Merry Widow, and countless others.

I saw every one of these — but without ever paying a cent. My father was an usher at a theater, so I could just walk in and take any seat I liked, even in the first row, only a few steps from the stage.

Here I came alive. When the houselights dimmed and the orchestra began the overture, when the curtain rose and I saw the huge stage bathed in brilliant light, my desire to be an actor became so overwhelming that tears welled to my eyes. How I longed to live my life among creative people: actors, writers, and composers!

But I knew this was an impossible dream. The next morning at eight, I would be back at my job, and my secret desire would remain buried in my heart.

☆ ☆ ☆

I was, perhaps, sixteen when my interest shifted from the make-believe world of operettas to the serious theater. The great dramas I saw touched my heart. They spoke of the things that move the human spirit, of compassion and friendship, of coldness and deceit, and of that rare gift: self-giving love.

It was my generation's great privilege to see performances by the giants of the dramatic stage, like Albert Bassermann and Alexander Moissi. Often I went to the stage door to watch the great ones emerge, smile at the cheering crowd, sign a few autographs, and get into their chauffeur-driven automobiles.

It was always close to midnight when I walked home through the dark and quiet city, dreaming of the day when I would stand on that stage.

☆ ☆ ☆

That day came unexpectedly! How? The theater announced auditions for young actors; I applied and was invited.

I stood before the bright footlights. From the dark of the orchestra, a voice asked, "Where do you come from?" I didn't know what he meant, so I said, "I come from home." I knew it was a stupid answer, but I didn't understand the question and didn't know what else to say.

He asked, "What have you prepared?" I started to recite one of the dramatic poems I knew. After a few lines, he interrupted, "Prepare something different and come again." Clearly, it was a polite way of turning me down.

On the way home, I pondered his question, "Where do you come from?" What could he have meant? Of what interest could it possibly be to him where I came from? Then the light dawned: All the other young people were probably students at some drama school, and he wanted to know at which school I studied.

A school? Ridiculous! Where would the Waldmanns find money for drama lessons? We often had difficulty paying the gas bill!

☆ ☆ ☆

My first love was a girl from Prague. She had come to Vienna to spend a few weeks with her aunt. The word was that her parents had sent her to Vienna to help her get over some disappointment in love.

Her family owned a large store in Prague, and my mother thought it would be nice if I could marry this girl. She knew of a poor young man who had married into a business and had become rich. She added, "It isn't necessary to be in love. You get to like each other after you are married."

Well, the girl was very pretty, and I liked her right from the start. We had a great time seeing all the movies and plays, and I enjoyed every minute with her. (The store in Prague never entered my mind.)

Then one day she announced that soon she would have to return to Prague. I realized then how much she had become part of my life and how much I would miss her. I brought her a few roses on her last evening in Vienna, and with a heavy heart, I said good-bye.

I slept very little that night. I rose before dawn and ran to her house. Perhaps I could see her once more or even accompany her to the train. But I was too late. She was gone. I walked back home, wrapped in gloom.

A few days later, the mailman brought a letter from her. It was heavily perfumed, and the contents revealed a shallowness and appalling lack of intelligence I had not detected when I looked at her pretty face. This discovery slowly but *definitely* ended my yearning for the girl from Prague.

☆ ☆ ☆

In the movies all the handsome, self-assured men lit cigarette after cigarette. So I started to smoke. I was sure it would give me poise. But I was wrong. All it gave me was a sick stomach.

Yet I persisted. I spent several weeks learning to smoke without getting green in the face. (After that, I spent twenty-one years getting rid of the addiction.)

☆ ☆ ☆

I was about seventeen when something strange began to happen: Girls often turned around for a second look when I passed them on the street. This made me quite conceited.

It also made me extremely conscious of my appearance. The perfect crease in my trousers and the correct tilt in the brim of my hat became matters of supreme importance. I spent endless hours in front of the mirror studying myself, and the more I studied, the more conceited I became.

I still have a snapshot of myself taken around that time. It shows me in topcoat and hat, leaning on a cane, my nose up in the air, a far-away, almost disdainful, look in my eyes. A perfect caption for this picture would be "Arrogance, thy name is Kurt."

1928

TOYING WITH SUICIDE

*A*t this point in my life, I thought I was a pretty wonderful fellow, but one evening I almost took my own life.

It had been an ordinary workday, no different from any other: my job no more demanding than usual, my fellow employee Ernest and his sarcasm no more annoying than usual.

I came home about seven and entered our apartment. It was empty. I expected that. My father was at his job in the theater, and my mother spent most of her evenings at a cousin's house, playing a penny ante game of cards.

I walked into the kitchen. It was spotlessly clean — and cold. (Everything at our house was always spotless, and most of our rooms were always cold. Coal cost money.) A vague feeling of depression came over me.

As I looked around the kitchen, my eyes fell on the table with the familiar threadbare oilcloth — and suddenly my life seemed just as threadbare: a life of well-scrubbed shabbiness — a life without meaning, without hope....

Walking over to the gas stove, I opened the jet. I heard the hissing sound of the escaping gas. I wondered how soon I would feel the first sign of drowsiness.

I thought of my parents; I pictured my mother wringing her hands in despair. I pushed the thought out of my mind. Then I saw one of my uncles shaking his head in disbelief. And then I saw Ernest, my sarcastic fellow worker. I saw his face broadening into an amused grin as he heard the news of my death.

THAT DID IT! No matter what, I was not going to give Ernest this enjoyment!

I walked over to the stove, shut the gas off, and left the apartment.

1929-1930

HOT TEMPER...
HARSH TRUTH

*O*n early 1929 I committed a foolish blunder: I quit my job. Why? My company was in a bit of financial difficulty, and in haste, I decided to get out before it was too late. (Too late for what? I wasn't really sure.)

I scanned the papers for a job opening in my line and soon found one. I went to apply, and there I committed blunder number two: I got greedy. I asked for *twice* the salary I had been receiving. To my amazement the boss hired me on the spot. Perhaps he was impressed by my counterfeited self-confidence. He didn't know how my knees were shaking.

I went home, rejoicing. In my mind I pictured all the things I would now be able to afford.

But the bubble soon burst. Within a few days, my future boss let me know, through a third person, that he had reconsidered, and if I wanted to stay in my old job...

But it was too late for that; I had already given notice. On February 15, I left the place which had been home for me during the last four and a half years, and the next morning I went to my new place of employment. The boss stood near the door. He looked at me and said, "Oh, it's you!" This was the beginning of the end.

Why didn't he dismiss me on the spot? Because a clause in Austrian law made this impossible. He could not terminate my employment before the thirtieth of June. He had to keep me and pay me for four and a half months.

But he was not one to give up easily. That afternoon he made the following proposal: He would give me a month's salary, I would sign away any further claim on him, and I would be free to leave at once and look for another job. I declined the offer.

That only made him more determined. He began to criticize everything I did and said, hoping to provoke me into quitting. I didn't fall for that either. That really irritated him.

One day, in an exceptionally foul mood, he picked on one of the apprentices, a skinny, timid fifteen-year-old. He began by screaming at the frightened boy. Then, at the height of his rage, he threw a heavy package at him, almost knocking him to the floor. The boy cried like a little child.

Then, with a look of fury in his eyes, he began to scream at me. Well, unfortunately I had — and still have — a very explosive temper, well-hidden but ever present. In a flash my blood reached its boiling point. I shouted in return, asking him how he had the audacity to raise his voice to me — he who had hired me away from a permanent job, only to throw me out on the street. He stared at me, turned, walked into his office, and shut the door.

In the back room was an old tailor hunched over his work. He smiled at me and whispered, "I was so happy when I heard you. In all the years I've been here, you're the only one who had the courage to stand up to him."

But it was a hollow victory. Only a few short weeks later, I received my last paycheck: Now I was unemployed. And this was only the beginning. I soon discovered that wherever I applied for a job and named my last boss as reference, smiles changed into blank stares, and doors closed in my face.

☆ ☆ ☆

The weeks and months slipped by, summer gave way to fall, and fall to winter — and still no job. Then I thought about going back to my first boss, to the place where I had quit after four and a half years. I would ask him to take me back.

It wasn't a happy thought. I dreaded meeting him face to face and admitting my stupidity, yet the longer I thought about it, the more hopeful I became. Surely, he would be forgiving. He would understand that, after all, I was only a silly youngster, that I had learned my lesson, and in the future I would make the most loyal employee.

One cold winter evening, I stood in the dark street near his place of business and waited for him. At last he came. I walked up to him and stammered something about being sorry and would he have an opening...

He looked straight into my eyes and said, "I run a place of business, not a birdhouse. You can't simply fly in and fly out anytime you like." Then he turned and walked away.

☆ ☆ ☆

YOUNG ADULTHOOD

☆ ☆ ☆

1930-1933

DOES GOD LISTEN?

*M*y friend Eugene had become a well-known comedian; he had a number of writers who supplied his material. I said to myself, if others could make a living by writing, why not I?

I wrote a piece and took it to Vienna's most famous entertainer. This man was, without exaggeration, the darling of Vienna. His name was a household word. His jovial smile greeted us from billboards all across the city.

I went to the theater where he performed and waited backstage. I could hear the sound of the piano, his well-known happy voice, and the usual storm of applause. But offstage he was a changed person. The famous smile was gone; his face was expressionless.

Timidly, I mumbled something as I handed him my piece. He glanced at it, and without looking at me, handed it back and said "No," and walked away.

Others were a little less famous and a lot more helpful. I remember especially Christine Giampietro, a great entertainer and a perfect lady. She took time to sit down with me and read my material. She said, "You have talent, but you are young, and your writing still needs a little more polish. But don't give up! Remember, you have talent."

So I continued to write and here and there sold a piece to lesser celebrities. It brought in some money, but not enough. I still needed a job.

My cousin Hans, the indomitable, came to my help. He was sales manager at a magazine distribution center; the company needed a bill collector. On his recommendation, I was hired. After a while they hired my father also. Now the Waldmanns were beginning to look forward to a worry-free life.

But it was too good to last. Within a year the company went out of business, and the Waldmanns were unemployed.

☆ ☆ ☆

The year was 1932, and Europe, too, was in the grip of the Great Depression. There were no jobs. I searched the papers, I asked anyone I could think of. Nothing. Nil.

Then one day the thought came to me: "I could ask God." And so I did. At the same time, I felt it wasn't fair to go to God only when I needed something. I had largely ignored him most of my life; I had never paid any attention to the numerous commandments of the Jewish faith. It seemed only fair that I should give something in return for what I expected. I knew that religious Jews did not smoke on the Sabbath. So, for two Saturdays I gave up my beloved cigarettes.

Then something unbelievable happened. One afternoon a young man rang our doorbell and offered me a job!

A JOB! Viennese, by the thousands, were lining up at the unemployment office, and *he came to our house* to offer me a job! He was with a publishing firm. They knew that I had worked for the magazine distribution center, and they wondered if I would like to do the same work for them.

It was a family-owned business, a small, homelike place. The owners were refined, educated people.

There was no doubt in my mind that this job was an answer to my prayer. My heart was full of gratitude, and I could only marvel at the generosity of God.

But, then, one day a book came into my hands, a philosophic work. It asked: Is there *really* a God who rewards the good and punishes evil? Can we picture a God, sitting in heaven, before him a gigantic book into which he writes all the good and bad things people do? Isn't the very idea absurd?

This sort of reasoning was new to me, and the more I thought about it, the more I felt inclined to agree with the author. Maybe he was right. Maybe there was no God after all.

But I said to myself, "I had just been so immensely grateful to God because he had given me this job. Why do I doubt?"

I wondered how others felt about God. I thought of my relatives. Many of them were successful people who led secure, well-regulated lives; they were people whose intelligence I admired — and they felt no need for God. They considered religion something "for the old folks."

Then there was the author of this philosophic work. He was far more educated than I. Surely, he knew what he was speaking of....

That didn't satisfy me, either. What if there *was* a God, and I turned my back on him?

Finally, this emotional roller coaster got too much for me, and I dropped the whole matter.

☆ ☆ ☆

My new job lasted about a year. Then the publishing firm, too, fell victim to the Depression — and I was once again unemployed.

I had a lot of time to think now — and think I did. I began to ask myself about the purpose of life. Was I put on this earth only to worry constantly about jobs and rent payments?

And what if I had a lot of money? Would I be happier then? Could I buy a worry-free life? Don't the rich sooner or later have to leave all their enjoyments and all their money behind?

For the first time in my life, I tried to look beyond my day-to-day existence, tried to discern some purpose in my life, some reason for my being here. For the first time in my life, I asked myself, "Why was I born?"

The answer came many months later when I had already forgotten that I had asked the question. I was walking along the Ringstrasse, the elegant boulevard which encircles the downtown area. Near the opera, I passed a sidewalk café. I glanced at the young men and women who sat there enjoying the afternoon sun. I felt a touch of sadness, wondering why I couldn't have a pleasant, carefree life as they had. At that moment a thought came into my mind. It said clearly, "You were born because God has a definite plan for you."

1934

STORM CLOUDS

OVER AUSTRIA

*I*t is very disconcerting to grow up in a country where the form of government changes every few years.

When I was born, Austria was a monarchy. At school the teacher gave each child a small picture of Emperor Karl and Empress Zita, and she pointed out to us "what beautiful, white hands" the young empress had.

When I was eight years old, the emperor and empress were gone; I heard people say that Austria was now a republic. All my uncles were Social Democrats and talked about improving the lot of the proletariat.

By the time I got to be a teenager, two opposing militias had sprung up in Austria (one fascistic, the other socialistic), each looking for an opportunity to topple the government. And my uncles were scolding me for not being a member of the Socialist Youth.

By 1934 — I was twenty-four then — Austria had become a republic in name only. The government began to suppress the Social Democrats, and when they, in turn, revolted, the government squelched the revolt by brutal force.

It all began one day in February. I had gone to visit my cousin Hans. He said to me, "Something is going on. There is trouble downtown near the government buildings." I said, "Let's go and see."

It was only a ten-minute walk from Hans's house to the bridge across the Danube Canal and into downtown. As we turned the corner and came near the bridge, we found ourselves staring at two machine guns pointed at us. The army had a barrier of barbed wire blocking any approach to the bridge and had cordoned off the entire downtown area.

During the next few days we heard sporadic gunfire. We were, of course, confined to our immediate neighborhood, and before long, food became scarce. One evening I stood in line outside a bakery, hoping to buy a loaf of bread. Suddenly, we heard something like the roar of cannons. Then there was silence.

When life in the city returned to normal, the terrible truth became known: A number of socialists had barricaded themselves in an apartment building, and the government had used cannons to put an end to the trouble — and the trouble-makers.

I went to see that house. Located on a side street in a workers' district, it was just an ordinary four-story building like many others in Vienna, except for one difference: In the center there was a gigantic hole. Two entire floors — and the people in them — had been blasted out of existence by artillery.

But this was only the beginning of trouble. Austrian Nazis, supported by Hitler's regime in next-door Germany, did their utmost to create disturbances and overthrow the Austrian government. Almost every day bombs exploded somewhere in Vienna.

On July 25, 1934, several Nazis, disguised as Vienna police, entered Chancellor Dollfuss's office, locked the door, and shot him. It was twenty-four hours before police could break down the door and arrest the assassins. During that time, Dollfuss lay on the floor, bleeding to death.

1934-1937

ACTOR – WRITER –

DIRECTOR

*T*he plot had failed; the Austrian government survived. Kurt von Schuschnigg became chancellor now, and we resumed our everyday lives, hoping that everything would be all right.

Of course, there *was* Hitler right across the border, but we made ourselves believe that he presented no real danger. After all, the Viennese were too intelligent, too cultured, to fall for this fellow with the funny mustache.

☆ ☆ ☆

As for myself, I had now decided to devote all my time to writing, and what followed were a few really happy years. I began to move among show people. One day I met Walter Lindenbaum, an exceptionally gifted comedy writer. Walter and I wrote an Abbott-and-Costello type routine for two young comedians. It was instantly successful and remained a favorite with audiences for a long time.

Then one lucky day I met Hans Hollander. Hans was young,

an outstanding pianist, and a good performer. I wrote some material for him, and after a while he and I began to perform together. We played some sketches, made good money, and had a lot of fun. It was pure enjoyment. But my greatest thrill came when I discovered that I could direct; I could transform a lifeless show into a sparkling success.

Here's how it happened: Hans informed me that he was running a weekend cabaret. He asked if I would like to come and see it and let him know what I thought of it?

Well, I came, I saw — and I found it mediocre. There were a number of acts following one another haphazardly, and the supposed climax was a duet which Hans sang with his partner, a pretty, young girl. It was a song about two sweethearts who had to part — never to see each other again. It was a sad song, but Hans and his partner smiled pleasantly as they sang. The audience responded with polite applause.

After the show, Hans asked how I liked it. I told him, "You need two people: a master of ceremonies and, above all, a director." His face fell. "Where can I find these people?" I said, "You found them; I'll be both."

Where did I get the courage to take on something I knew nothing about? I don't know, but somehow I felt — and felt with certainty — that I could make this show come alive.

We went to work the next Monday morning, and we rehearsed all week. The first thing we tackled was the duet. It was obvious to me the two did not *feel* the sadness of the song: The piano was too loud and their faces too happy. Yet this was rather easily corrected. After a few tries the words began to ring true.

But there was still something about it that bothered me, something that wasn't right. For a long while, I couldn't put my finger on it. Then it hit me: The song spoke of evening twilight, yet the stage looked like high noon. I went backstage and studied the lighting; there I found my answer.

☆ ☆ ☆

The evening of the first performance came. I was emcee, introduced the various acts, told a few amusing stories, and watched the audience come alive. It was good to see all these smiling faces. Hans, his partner, and I played some sketches, and all of us — performers and audience alike — had a lot of fun. It was truly an enjoyable evening.

Finally, the moment for the duet came — the song about the two sweethearts who had to part forever. Now we would find out if my assumed directing skills made an iota of difference. At the very last minute, I had another idea: I whispered a few words to the violinist, who followed me backstage, and we were ready to begin.

The curtain slowly opened on a semidark stage. The piano softly intoned the haunting melody, joined a moment later by the muted violin. Two hushed voices began to sing the heart-rending ballad.

In the song, evening twilight gave way to the dark of night; the stage also grew darker and darker until only a shimmer of blue light remained. As the two lovers whispered their last good-bye and the melody faded, the audience sat spellbound in almost total darkness and absolute silence.

A second later I flooded the stage with brilliant light, and I heard an outburst of applause as I had heard only a few times in my life, at performances of some of the greatest dramatic actors.

Some people who had seen the show the week before asked Hans, "What have you done? It's almost the same show as last week, but it's so much better! *What have you done?*" Hans beamed with happiness, and I knew that I had found a new love: DIRECTING! I discovered that I had the gift to stir the emotions of an audience — that I could make people feel. And I began to dream of glorious things to come....

☆ ☆ ☆

I did not dream long. Within a few months, my whole world collapsed.

EARLY 1938

AUSTRIA ON THE BRINK

*I*n Vienna, the Nazis began to make their presence felt. Death and devastation, caused by bombs, became the order of the day.

The German army, with its panzer divisions, stood at the Austrian border, ready to overrun little Austria and its pitifully small army.

Hitler invited Austrian Chancellor Schuschnigg to a meeting. There Schuschnigg was forced to agree to take the Nazi Seyss-Inquart into his cabinet as minister of the interior.

This, of course, meant the end of Austria's independence. For the Jews of Austria, it created a specter of unknown and unimaginable terrors.

But, then, into the midst of this gloom and despair, there came wonderful, encouraging news: Chancellor Schuschnigg ordered a plebiscite to let the Austrian people decide whether they wanted to remain citizens of a free Austria or live under Hitler's rule.

At last we dared to hope again. Surely, we said, the Austrian people would make the right choice.

But the people never had a chance to choose. It was March 11, 1938 — two days *before* the expected plebiscite....

☆ ☆ ☆

HITLER

☆ ☆ ☆

MARCH 11, 1938
THE END OF AUSTRIA

A pall of gloom seemed to hang over the city of Vienna. Even the sky was a dreary gray. My heart was heavy, and my brain was numb with fear of the unknown. Would Austria remain free or be swallowed up by Hitler's Germany? In two days we would know. In two days the people of Austria would cast their ballots.

I spent a completely unproductive day. How could I possibly write comedy? How could I think funny thoughts? I was like a man waiting for sentence to be pronounced.

In the evening I had an appointment with a singer who had asked me to do some work for her. She and her family lived in the downtown section of Vienna.

We had barely begun to work when we heard shouting in the street. We listened. There it was again — clear and unmistakable. The next moment her family, panic in their eyes, burst into the room. "Schuschnigg has been arrested! He spoke on the radio…the Nazis took over the radio station!"

I jumped up and ran down the stairs. Cautiously, I put my head out the door. A howling mob surged up the sidewalk toward me. There was no escape, except…right across the street there was a house that through its courtyard, connected with another house in the next block. My father had shown me this shortcut when I was a boy. This was my escape!

I dashed across the street, through the two adjoining buildings, and a few seconds later I was on a quiet side street. From there I made my way home by means of the little streets and narrow passageways I knew so well.

I reached our apartment building, raced up the stairs, and there on the fourth floor stood a number of Jewish tenants, my mother among them. Their faces were ashen; their eyes wide with fear. I told them what I had seen and heard. Then we silently went back to our apartments. It was almost morning before I drifted off to sleep.

THE MORNING AFTER...
A STRANGE CITY

*A*wakened by an unfamiliar noise, I jumped out of bed and ran to the window and saw German bombers circling the city — a harsh reminder that Austria was a conquered land.

I couldn't believe my eyes! Giant banners, displaying the swastika, were everywhere. The street was full of people, some of them Nazi storm troopers.

I asked myself, how could the city have changed so drastically overnight? Then the frightening realization came to me: The takeover of Austria obviously had been well prepared from within; evidently, many of the people among whom we lived were Hitler's fifth column.

Dressing quickly, I ran outside. There was a small grocery store across the street. In six-foot letters the word *JEW* had been painted across its window — an open invitation to vandalize, plunder, or even kill.

A column of storm troopers came marching down the street, their boots clattering against the cobblestone pavement. As they marched, they sang, "...when the blood of Jews runs from our knives, then we feel twice as good."

SPRING 1938

DOES GOD TAKE CARE

OF THE SPARROWS?

*J*ews had become fair game. Two Nazis walked into the neighborhood pharmacy and told the Jewish owner to get out — no explanation given, no compensation offered. Just "Take your hat and coat and get out!"

I had an uncle who for many years held an important position in a large manufacturing firm. One morning he was barred from entering the plant. The doorman was very apologetic, "I am sorry, sir. I have instructions not to let you in." The president of the same firm was thrown out and replaced by a stock clerk.

Jews everywhere lost jobs, businesses, possessions — and often more. Many disappeared. Some were dragged out of their beds in the middle of the night. One night I heard the sound of a sledgehammer breaking a door down. I don't know who was taken. One did not ask questions.

☆ ☆ ☆

My cousin Hans, through a friend in Zurich, obtained a visa to Switzerland. Lucky Hans! One evening his parents and I accompanied him to the railroad station. As the train pulled out, Hans waved good-bye and tears came to my eyes. I wasn't crying for Hans, who was traveling toward freedom, I cried for myself, who stayed behind. We left the station and walked home through the dark, deserted streets. A small group of storm troopers marched by, and suddenly I had the sinking feeling that for me there was no way out; my end would come somewhere in some dark, deserted place, just like this.

☆ ☆ ☆

The days dragged on — days of gloom and hopelessness. One afternoon I looked out the window and saw some sparrows hopping around, looking for a few morsels of food. For a fleeting moment, I envied those little birds. How carefree they were! How easily they could fly across borders....

A question came to my mind: "Does God take care of the sparrows?" How else could they find their food on the stone pavements of the city? And — if he takes care of them — perhaps he will help me, too! For the first time, I saw a glimmer of hope, and my heart felt a little lighter.

☆ ☆ ☆

A few days later I walked across the street to visit the parents of Eugene. (Eugene, you may remember, was a comedian, and he happened to be on engagement in Prague.) A young man walked only a few steps ahead of me. An older man came up to him and quietly asked, "Are you a Jew?" He answered, "Yes." The older man said, "Keep your mouth shut and get into that wagon across the street." Out of the corner of my eye, I spotted a police wagon.

At that moment, I reached Eugene's house and quickly disappeared through the doorway. Eugene's father was home alone. A few minutes later, Eugene's mother burst into the apartment, her eyes wide with fear. "You know what Mrs. Schwarz told me? Two young men were walking near our house. One of them was arrested and the other got white in the face and hid in our house!"

"Yes," I replied, "I know. I am the young man who got white in the face."

SUMMER 1938

LONG JOURNEY

INTO NOWHERE

There was no doubt that if I wanted to stay alive, I had to get out of Austria. But how? Some Jews had relatives in Palestine or America; I had no one. Some crawled across borders in the dark of night; I was too cowardly to try that. I just didn't know what to do.

Then one evening my cousin Paul, Hans's younger brother, said he heard about an easy way to get into Switzerland.

He had my immediate attention. "Switzerland? How? Tell me!"

"Well, the police of Cologne, in cooperation with the Jewish community…"

"Now wait a moment! German police and the Jewish community?…"

"That's what I heard. They are exchanging Austrian passports for German passports, which in turn can be used to obtain Swiss visas."

Now that was about the silliest thing I had heard in a long

time! Germans helping Jews escape from the Germans! I wouldn't give it another thought!

On the other hand — what if it *was* true? What if I missed a chance — the only chance I really had?

My young cousin asked, "Will you go?"

"Sure, I'll go. I have to try something — *anything.* "

Then he begged me: "Will you take me along?"

"Yes, with your father's permission." (Paul was only eighteen; I was twenty-eight.)

On the following day, he asked if I would also take along his friend Kurt.

"Sure, I'll take Kurt, too."

One Friday afternoon we climbed aboard the train to Cologne. Each of us carried not much more than a toothbrush and a comb; but we did have an endless supply of cheese sandwiches. It was a five-hundred-mile, eighteen-hour journey, and we spent it sitting on the hard wooden benches of our compartment, my two companions more asleep than awake. I spent much of the time thinking of the people I would have to meet the next day, and I dreamed of the happy moment when we would get our Swiss visas and cross the border into freedom.

It was seven o'clock on Saturday morning when the train pulled into the Cologne station. We walked across the street for a cup of coffee then set out to find the office of the Jewish community.

There I had a pleasant surprise: The Jewish community of Vienna had wired them on my behalf. (I had asked for their help.) But then came the bad news: We were too late.

"The police don't do it anymore," the lady explained. "Yes, they helped some Austrian Jews, but they stopped it last Wednesday. You are three days late."

I asked, "What can we do?"

"Go back to Vienna."

☆ ☆ ☆

My two companions and I stood outside the building, nonplused. Just then the door opened and a man came out. He said, "I wanted to talk to the president, but he is not at the office today." An idea shot into my head. I asked, "Do you know the *name* of the president?" He did.

My companions looked puzzled. I explained, "I'll go to the president's home and ask him to help us. Let's find a phone book." The name was listed — in fact, there were five people by that name. But that was no problem. I would take the streetcar to each of the five until I found the right one.

I told my companions I would meet them in the evening, and I started out. Of the five, only three were at home. One was an old woman; the second opened the door and said, "Heil Hitler! What do you wish?" But the last address was that of the president of the Jewish community. It was four o'clock in the afternoon when I reached his home.

I apologized for intruding on his privacy. He listened to me with great interest. Then he put his hand on my shoulder and said, "I will do my best to help you. I will phone some people this evening. Come and see me at the office early Monday morning." I was overwhelmed with happiness, and I poured out my thanks to him.

My two companions were jubilant when they heard the wonderful news. We spent a happy Sunday sightseeing. (Cologne is a beautiful city.) We could hardly believe our good fortune. Tomorrow we would get our German passports; then we'd go to the Swiss consulate for our visas, and finally to Switzerland and freedom.

Monday morning at eight we were outside the office of the Jewish community. From a distance I saw the president coming. When he spotted me, he waved, "Too late! Too late! I just had a phone call from the Swiss consul. He has new instructions effective today. He cannot issue any more visas. So, even if the police would give you a German passport, it would be useless. I am very sorry...." He smiled regretfully and walked into the building.

This was a crushing blow! We stood around debating what to do next. None of us wanted to go back to Vienna. My cousin thought maybe we could try to get into Czechoslovakia. I didn't like the idea. Too close to Communist Russia. I wanted to go west, not east. Then his friend mentioned he had heard someone say that the Swiss consul in Stuttgart was helping Jews. We all said, "Let's go to Stuttgart," and we trudged off to the railroad station.

☆ ☆ ☆

There was no direct train to Stuttgart; we faced a five-hour layover in Frankfurt. It was nine o'clock in the evening when we arrived in Frankfurt — and we were starved! But every restaurant we saw had a large sign at the door: *Juden verboten* (No Jews allowed.)

I don't know how long we walked the streets until we found a small automat — and there was no *Juden verboten* at the door! We entered, and we ate and ate....I started with chocolate cake, followed by two sandwiches, followed by apple strudel. We spent an hour in that place, and as we walked out I glanced back. There in a corner of a window was a small sign: *Juden verboten!*

Back at the railroad station, we found the waiting room closed, so we sat on a bench near the track. It was cold and dark — the only light provided by a large clock in the distance. It showed eleven o'clock. Our train was due at two in the morning.

When at last it came, we climbed aboard, barely awake. We collapsed on the hard wooden bench and closed our eyes. If only we could sleep a few hours! But this was not to be. In the compartment were a soldier and a middle-aged civilian. The civilian talked incessantly, about the weather, about his family, about the train service....Nobody paid any attention, but he talked for seven hours — all the way to Stuttgart.

It was nine o'clock in the morning when we arrived — completely exhausted. We managed to find the Swiss consulate, but all we got was a polite "Sorry. No visas, except for business purposes." (And for this we had traveled all the way to Stuttgart.)

My two companions looked wilted. I said, "Let's find the Jewish community and see if they have any advice." It was a small office — only one lady behind a desk. I began, "We are three Jews from Vienna..." and she continued, "...and you want to go back to Vienna." My brain wanted to say "No," but my mouth said "Yes." I knew I had come to the end of my strength. We had dinner at an exceptionally pleasant restaurant, and then we picked up our tickets for the return trip — all at the community's expense.

Once on the train I could think of only one thing: Tomorrow I'll sleep in my own bed...I'll sleep...sleep...

LATE SUMMER –
EARLY FALL 1938
THE DISILLUSIONED NAZI

*O*ur mailman was an unusually warm and pleasant person. He always greeted me with a genuine smile and a kind word. Imagine my shock when one day I saw him wearing a storm trooper's uniform. As we passed on the street, he looked right through me.

A few weeks later we met again. This time he was back in his mailman's outfit, and he wanted to talk. He told me how disillusioned he was. "They promised us a great country. All they do is ship food from Austria to Germany. Every night while people sleep, carloads of food leave for Germany." He paused for a few moments before saying: "And the poor Jews! It's a disgrace! An animal has more protection than a Jew." I just listened. I wouldn't dare open my mouth. Could I trust him? Was he perhaps trying to trick me into saying something against the regime?

I received my answer only a few days later. We met again. In fact, he spotted me half a block away, and he eagerly called me. As I stood near him, he let his fingers run through a stack of letters and under his breath said, "Stay home tomorrow. They'll be arresting as many Jews as they can find." Then he looked up and in a loud voice said, "No, I don't have any mail for you today."

☆ ☆ ☆

In the twenty-eight years of my life, I had hardly ever been to synagogue — surely not more than a dozen times. Now, out of the clear sky, I decided to go *every day*. I had — at last — come to realize that God was my only hope.

No doubt, attending synagogue was risky. How easily the Nazis could have picked me up as I left at the end of services. Yet that didn't stop me.

Evening after evening I stood there listening to the rabbi and the men in the congregation recite the Hebrew prayers. I couldn't join in with them, but I was certain that God accepted my voiceless presence as my plea for help.

☆ ☆ ☆

Practically every Jew in Vienna studied English. We all hoped to go to America. I dug out my old English books and started again from scratch. It all came back very quickly.

One day I met a girl. She asked me the question all Viennese Jews were asking one another, "Who is your English teacher?"

"Nobody. I'm teaching myself."

"Will you teach me? My teacher went to America."

"Oh, heavens! I can't do that! I never taught anybody in my life."

"I bet you could! I'll pay you the same as I paid my last teacher."

Reluctantly, I agreed to try. She was so pleased that she recommended me to her cousin, and the cousin to a friend, and before I knew it, I had about a dozen students. I made good money, and — best of all — I improved my knowledge of

English by trying to find simple explanations to my students' vexing problems.

I think of my students often. They were so eager to prepare themselves for a new life in a new land. I wonder how many of them reached their haven.

NOVEMBER 10, 1938
O GOD, SAVE ME!

*T*his was the day when death stared me in the face. I left the house early in the morning, a little after eight o'clock. (I was taking a course then, hoping to acquire a skill that would help me to start anew in some other country.)

I had walked only a block or so when an elderly lady stopped me. "You are Mr. Waldmann, aren't you?"

"Yes, I am."

"You don't know me; I know your mother." She looked extremely worried. "Please, go back home. Something terrible is happening. They are arresting Jews."

I shrugged it off. "Nothing is going to happen to me." I thanked her for her concern and went on my way.

At the teacher's home were three other students. We had barely begun our lesson when the phone rang. It was the wife of one of the men. She begged him to come home immediately. "Some terrible things are going on." He left in great haste. The other two men looked apprehensive, and a few minutes later they, too, were gone.

I was alone with the teacher and his wife. They assured me, "You can stay with us as long as you want; you'll be safe here.

The caretaker in our building is a member of the Party, and he won't let anyone hurt his Jewish tenants." It was a very sincere offer, but how long could I stay cooped up? I *had* to get home to see what was happening. I thanked them and then I left.

Downstairs, I cautiously put my head out the door. The street was empty — no people, no traffic. In the far distance, I saw two thugs carrying heavy clubs, obviously looking for someone to attack. They were coming in my direction. I quickly walked around the corner and hopped on the first streetcar that came along, not caring where it went.

After zigzagging the city, at last I came into my neighborhood with its predominantly Jewish population. Here the streets were totally deserted — no sign of life anywhere.

I got off at my stop and walked to the corner. A large open truck was parked at the curb. Standing in it were twenty or thirty men and women — obviously on their way to the death camps. I quickly passed without raising my head.

I reached the corner and turned into my street. I had two long blocks ahead of me before I would be home. I walked as fast as I could without running. Halfway down the block, the street curved to the right. I passed that spot, and there — a stone's throw away — I saw our house! In another minute or less, I would be safely home.

At that moment, two storm troopers turned the corner, stopped within a few feet of our door, and stood there watching me. There was nobody in the street except the three of us.

I felt the blood drain from my face, and my mind began to race. I continued to walk toward them. I approached one of the houses and was severely tempted to hide in it. But I knew they would find me there. I came to the next house. Once again I rejected the same temptation. I was still walking — right into the grasp of the waiting Nazis. My heart pounded like a hammer, and I pleaded with God to help me.

At that instant it came to me what I must do: I put my hands into my pockets, put a smile on my face, and whistling a tune, marched past the two Nazis straight into our house, shutting the door behind me.

But I was not yet safe. Out of the corner of my eye, I saw one of the Nazis following me. I knew he could see me through the small window in the door. I walked very slowly down the corridor, as if I didn't have a worry in the world. Then I turned the corner toward the stairs. Now he couldn't see me anymore. I hastily pressed the bell to our apartment and raced up the five floors.

My mother had the door open for me. She said my face was as white as a sheet.

SPRING 1939
A LETTER FROM
AMERICA!

*O*f course, Jewish newspapers were forbidden in Nazi Austria. However, some courageous souls published a Jewish *underground* paper. It was printed on tissue paper, had only four pages, and was so small that we could easily fold it and put it into our shirt pockets.

One day this paper carried a small advertisement from a Jewish man, far out of the city. It read, "My cousin John X lives in Chicago. Can you help me find his address?"

I knew instantly I had to try to help this man. He lived far from the city and from any source of information, while I could easily go to the United States Consulate and look up his cousin's address in the Chicago phone book. (The U.S. Consulate in Vienna had opened one of their rooms to the general public, and there they had placed phone books of many American cities at our disposal. Only God knows how many lives they saved by this simple act of kindness.)

The small room was very crowded. It took awhile before I got hold of the Chicago book. Unfortunately, "cousin John" was not listed. Disappointed, I turned to leave; but then out of mere curiosity, I looked to see if there were any Waldmanns in Chicago. *I couldn't believe my eyes! There were dozens of them!*

I wondered: "Could some of these be my distant relatives? Could I write to them and ask for help?" I copied the addresses of eight or ten Waldmanns with Jewish-sounding first names, and then I left.

At home, I first wrote to the man whose ad had appeared in the paper and gave him the disheartening news: I couldn't find his cousin's address. Next, I sent letters to each of the Chicago Waldmanns.

A couple of months passed. Nothing happened until one glorious day, I saw my friend, the mailman, coming down the street. He waved to me and shouted, "A letter from America! A letter from America!" High in his hand he held that precious piece of paper that became my open door to freedom. One of the Chicago Waldmanns had set the wheels in motion. *And that man was not a Jew.*

☆ ☆ ☆

Now to get a passport! Simple? Not in Nazi Austria. It involved getting an endless number of documents before I could even apply for a passport. It meant endless hours of standing in line. And I do mean STANDING. I dared not turn around, talk to any one, or lean against a wall. I stood — silently and motionlessly — not wanting to draw attention to myself because I was dealing with people who had power over my very life.

At last I was ready to go to the passport office. I arrived at eight o'clock one morning. A sixteen-year-old in a storm trooper's uniform stood outside the building. As I came near him, he cursed me and pushed me, so that I almost fell. Inside, there was the inevitable line of people. It filled a broad staircase as far as I could see, to the second floor and beyond. After slowly inching my way along, I almost reached the third floor when a bell rang (it was noon) and someone shouted, "That's all! Everybody go home. Come back tomorrow."

The next morning I got there an hour earlier. I was relieved to see that the sixteen-year-old wasn't there, but outside the building there was a line two blocks long. At eight o'clock the line began to move — the door had been opened — and I slowly made my way around the corner, into the building, and up the staircase until I reached the third floor. Here in a long, narrow corridor were the passport offices. But the corridor was roped off, and the rope was guarded by another sixteen-year-old Nazi. Every ten minutes or so, he opened it and let a few people through — until, at long last, I was the first person in front of the rope. *I would be the next one in.* But at that very moment the bell rang, and the young boy shouted, "Everybody go home!"

For a split second I deliberated what to do. Then I dropped my handkerchief, bent down to get it, and when I stood up, I was *on the inside of the rope.* I walked very slowly down the corridor, entered one of the offices, and came out ten minutes later *with my passport.*

☆ ☆ ☆

I did not waste any time. The very next day I made application at the United States Consulate, and soon I held in my hand the key to freedom: my American visa.

Now all doors opened to me. I obtained, in rapid succession, visas for passage through England, France, and Switzerland. The dream had become reality.

SUMMER 1939

A LETTER FROM THE

WAR DEPARTMENT

*O*ne morning our mailbox contained a letter ordering me to report for induction into the army! Good God! My departure from Austria was only a few weeks away, and now this!

The induction center was full of gloomy young men, many of them my former classmates. Two young officers lined us up; then a stout major came and made a short speech. He explained what an honor it was to have been called upon to defend the fatherland.

Then someone shouted, "Are there any Jews here? Follow me." About eight or ten of us lined up behind him. He took us to a small room, told us to wait, and closed the door. We stood in a corner, barely speaking. We didn't know what they would do to us. A half hour later someone opened the door and said, "Oh, these are the Jews!" and closed it again. We waited. A half hour? an hour? It was an eternity.

At last a man came in. In his hand were several small sheets of green paper. These, he explained, were documents showing that we were excused from army service. He added, "If you are leaving the country, you'll have to show this at the border. Without it, you won't be permitted to leave." Then he told us we could go home.

My paper read, "The Jew Kurt Waldmann is unworthy to bear arms in defense of the fatherland and is excluded from military service." (My heart went out to my classmates who had been found "worthy" to give their young lives for the fatherland.)

☆ ☆ ☆

It became more apparent each day that Hitler was preparing the minds of the people for war. The government-controlled press began to blare insults at many neighboring countries. I remember especially one headline that called the Russian people "uncivilized barbarians." However, two days later the same newspaper declared that the Russians were a "sensitive and peace-loving people." (What caused this sudden, rather clumsy turnabout? Hitler had just signed a nonaggression pact with Russia.)

My departure from Vienna was set for July 25, and I was grateful for every day that brought me closer to that date. I knew if war should break out while I was inside Austria, I would not go to America — my destination would be the death camp.

☆ ☆ ☆

JOURNEY TO AMERICA

☆ ☆ ☆

JULY 25, 1939

GOOD-BYE TO VIENNA

The day I had so anxiously awaited finally came.

Shortly after noon I packed a few things into a small grip (my luggage had been sent ahead to Switzerland). Then I went to say good-bye to my father. He was seventy years old, and I knew I would never see him again. He definitely did not want to travel anywhere. He wanted to live out his life in Vienna. He was sure the Nazis wouldn't bother an old man. (The future proved how wrong he was.)

I picked up my grip and opened the door. My mother was at my side. Just then I remembered that I still had the keys to the apartment in my pocket. I put them on a little table and said to myself, "I won't need these anymore." A momentary feeling of intense sadness came over me. I realized that I would never again see the home of my childhood.

My mother walked to the stairs with me. I kissed her a last time — and I raced down at top speed. I knew her eyes were following me, but I did not look back. I did not want to see her tears.

☆ ☆ ☆

At the railroad station, I met a young couple I knew; we discovered that the three of us had booked passage to America on the same ship, and we happily decided to travel together.

The train slowly made its way westward, laboriously climbing through the Austrian Alps with their snow-covered peaks glistening in the setting sun. I had never seen such beauty before. But my mind was not on nature's splendor; my thoughts were with my mother, who had begged me to help her escape from the Nazis. What would I be able to do for her? What would America be like?

I closed my eyes and tried to rest my weary brain.

JULY 26, 1939
MY DEAR FRIEND,
THIS IS A *FREE*
COUNTRY!

*M*orning came and we were again traveling on level ground, the train moving at full speed. Suddenly, it slowed and came to a halt. I looked outside. There was no station, only a two-story building with a giant flag displaying the dreaded swastika.

I got up to look out the window to see why we had stopped. Then two SS men came aboard and locked the doors of the car. I hurried back to my seat. All conversation stopped instantly. The two men moved through the car checking luggage and passports. An old, familiar paralyzing fear crept into my heart. I had heard of people who were taken off the train at the border and sent to a concentration camp for some so-called "crime." (We were not allowed to take more than ten American dollars out of the country. We were forbidden to take with us anything of *any* value, even a gold ring or a small piece of jewelry.)

One of the Nazis came to me and barked, "Passport!" I handed it to him together with the green slip showing that I was excluded from army service. Then he demanded, "Luggage!" I pointed at the little grip in the luggage rack above my head. He glanced at it and moved on to my two friends.

They carried with them eight assorted pieces of luggage. The SS man rummaged through each piece. When he finally left, my friends had the chore of repacking their belongings.

It was perhaps a half hour since the two SS men had come aboard. At last they unlocked the doors and got off.

The train began to crawl, and after a few yards, it stopped again. A few of us got up to see what was happening. Outside there was a small house and on it a red flag with a white cross in its center.

Someone asked, "Is that the Swiss flag?"

Another answered, "It is! It is!" And then he shouted, "We're in Switzerland! We're in Switzerland!"

I stood at the window and stared at that beautiful flag which told me I had left the threat of torture and death behind. My eyes filled with tears, tears of happiness and gratitude.

Two Swiss custom officials came aboard. Smilingly, they said, "Good morning! Anything to declare?" There was no response. They said, "Have a good journey!" And they were gone.

The train now swiftly moved through a landscape of lush, green meadows amid countless lakes. I remained standing at the window, my eyes glued to the unbelievable beauty of the Swiss countryside, my heart overflowing with the pure joy of being alive.

☆ ☆ ☆

We arrived at Zurich, the first stopover on our journey. I took my grip and helped my friends with their mountain of luggage. We walked along the track toward the station building. At the door we put all the luggage down and searched our pockets for our tickets, ready to present them upon request. But the door was wide open, and there was nobody there to check our tickets. We looked at one another and said, "What a sloppy way to run a railroad!"

We walked into the station building and looked for the office where we could obtain permission to interrupt our journey. An old conductor came along. I asked him, "Where can we get permission…"

He looked astonished. "Permission? Permission for what?"

"We want to spend four days in Zurich, and…"

"Do you have your tickets?"

"Yes, we have tickets from Vienna to Paris."

"Do you have visas?"

"Yes."

"Well, then stay and enjoy yourselves!"

I was still not convinced. I started, "But…"

He shook his head at me, "My dear friend, you came from Austria. THIS is a FREE country!"

JULY–AUGUST 1939
HOW GOD LOST OUT
TO MRS. GOLDFARB

I lived twenty-nine years in Vienna and only four days in Zurich, but surprisingly, I'm homesick for Zurich! It was love at first sight! What appealed to me was the beauty of the city and the behavior of its residents.

One day on the street, I heard the screeching of brakes. A streetcar and an automobile had nearly collided. The motorman and the driver both jumped out and ran toward each other. I expected them to start shouting and hurling insults at each other, as I had heard hundreds of times in Vienna. Instead, the motorman said, "It was entirely my fault!" But the driver insisted, "No, not at all! I should have been more careful."

Another time I saw a young man in a business suit walking down the street. On his right shoulder he carried a rifle — yes, a rifle — and on his left shoulder a steel helmet. It was later explained to me that every able-bodied man in Switzerland was inducted into the army and had his uniform, his rifle, and ammunition at home so that in case of an attack from outside the army could stand in a half hour.

My amazement knew no bounds. I came from a country where, even under "normal" conditions, the authorities nursed a strong distrust of the population. Yet here the government *armed* the population for its own protection. This was, indeed, as the old conductor had said, a free country.

July 28 was a Friday, the beginning of the Sabbath, and I thought my two friends and I should go to synagogue to thank God for having saved our lives. But my friends had an appointment to visit a Mrs. Goldfarb whom they knew from Vienna, and I, too, was invited.

I suggested, "Couldn't we visit Mrs. Goldfarb tomorrow and go to synagogue tonight? After all, it's our first Sabbath in freedom!"

My friend merely looked at me out of the corner of his eye and said, "How do you like that? Mrs. Goldfarb expects us, and he wants to go to synagogue to thank God!"

I'm ashamed to say I gave in without a struggle. I spent a forgettable evening at Mrs. Goldfarb's.

☆ ☆ ☆

July 30 came; it was time to leave Zurich and move on to Paris. Here we had the unique experience of ordering in restaurants from menus we couldn't read — simply by pointing a finger at some dish and saying, "This." Once my friend thought we were being overcharged. He decided not to pay the bill but to call the police. I quietly asked him, "How would you call the police since you don't speak French? And how would you *talk* to the police?" He paid the bill.

During our stay in Paris, of course, we saw the magnificent boulevards, rode to the top of the Eiffel Tower, used the intelligently designed subway system, and saw one of the *Follies,* a French revue.

Once I managed to throw an entire police station into a tizzy. We needed some information. I walked in and, remembering my two years of French lessons, asked, *"Parlez vous Anglais?"* (Do you speak English?) For obvious reasons, I did not want to use German.

The sergeant was taking roll call, but at my question they all began to run around, looking out the window and the door, muttering, *"Anglais! Anglais!"* Finally one of them conveyed to me that there was a man who spoke English, and he would be back in *"Une minute."* And he kept repeating, *"Une minute! Une minute!"*

The policeman came; he walked several blocks with us until he found the person for whom we were looking. I thanked him by using the other two French words I remembered, *"Merci beaucoup!"* and came away with a very warm feeling about Parisians.

☆ ☆ ☆

Stately London was our next stop. We stayed only one day, but long enough for me to see my Viennese cousin, who surprised me with a delightful Viennese dinner.

The next day the train took us to Liverpool and to the ship. The date was August 5, 1939, my last day on European soil.

AUGUST 5-14, 1939
NO SEASICKNESS
FOR ME!

*T*he ship was the *Scythia,* one of the Cunard Line's smaller vessels — if any ocean liner can be called "small." It was a floating hotel with a ballroom and a variety of shops that catered to the passengers' needs.

My cabin was at the very bottom of the ship. It was the size of a closet — with just enough room for a narrow bed and an even narrower walking space.

My father had warned me about seasickness — he had been to America and back — and he had advised me to drink some whiskey at the first sign of dizziness. That would take care of it.

We had smooth sailing the first two days. I wandered up and down the ship, saw how the first-class passengers lived, played some deck games, and just enjoyed life.

On the morning of the third day, it hit me. When I awoke, I turned on the light. Lying there flat on my back, I saw the light riding around the ceiling in a large circle. "Aha!" I said, "I'll fix that!" I stared at the light until the circles got smaller and smaller, and the light finally returned to its place in the center of the ceiling.

I got out of bed and promptly flew against the wall. I said, "This is it! Time for the whiskey!" I opened the bottle I had bought in London and took a swallow.

Now, dizzy or not, I had to get to the bathroom. I had with me my shaving utensils, comb and brush, toothpaste and toothbrush, and a glass as I climbed four steep flights of stairs to the bathroom for third-class passengers.

My chores completed, I approached the stairs. At that moment the ship swayed, causing me to stumble. Everything fell out of my hands and went bouncing down the stairs — my body tumbling behind. The glass broke and I landed with a thud. Two stewards came running to pick up the broken glass — and me with my shattered vanity.

Next I ran head-on into the ship's interpreter, a short Hungarian Jew. (We had become acquainted on the first day of the journey; he had found out that I knew some English and had asked me to help him translate the menus for the many Germans and Austrians on board.)

He looked at me. "You are seasick! I'll tell you what you must do. Go to the dining room and eat as much as you can. Yes, I know you can't stand the thought of food. But *you must do what I tell you,* and you'll never be seasick again." He saw my hesitation and added, "Trust me. I have spent nine years on the Atlantic."

Well, I listened to the voice of experience. I was the *only* passenger in that vast dining room, and when I came out, my seasickness had vanished. I walked along the deck in that gorgeous sunshine. I had the whole ship to myself.

My two friends and the rest of the passengers were lying in their beds moaning and wishing that they "could die!" But after a couple of days, they all recovered, and the ship was again full of activity and laughter.

☆ ☆ ☆

Life aboard an ocean liner is a fairy-tale existence: eating, sleeping, playing — and romancing. I, too, had a few invitations to "sail together to that distant port." But I was determined to stay clear of any entanglement. I wanted to arrive in America alone, unattached — free to chart my own course.

☆ ☆ ☆

MY NEW COUNTRY

☆ ☆ ☆

AUGUST 14, 1939

A WONDERLAND

*T*his was the scheduled day for arrival in New York. I packed my few belongings early in the morning and spent the rest of the day wandering about the deck, hoping to catch a glimpse of my new country. But there was nothing — only the vast ocean.

At five in the afternoon, the call for dinner sounded. The waiters had just served the first course when someone put his head in the door and shouted, "You can see the Statue of Liberty!" In less than a minute, the large dining room emptied. I went up on deck with the others to stare at that beautiful, majestic lady silently welcoming me to my new home. I remained glued to the rail, wondering what my new country would be like, what life in America would hold for me.

My thoughts were suddenly interrupted when, down on the pier, I saw my cousin Hans, his wife Liesl, and Liesl's family. I nearly exploded with joy. I raced down countless flights of steps to my cabin, grabbed my suitcase, raced up again to the deck, and down the gangplank into their open arms.

Amid happy chatter, we piled into an automobile and drove through unbelievably crowded streets to their home. (I had never seen so many people and cars in my whole life!) We arrived at the house, and to my surprise it was a two-story building. I had thought that everybody in America lived in skyscrapers!

They lived in an apartment on the second floor, six of them, and they took me in — God bless them — as number seven. I wandered into the kitchen, and there I found things which to me bordered on the impossible: a gas stove that could be lighted *without using a match,* a faucet that discharged *hot* water, and a box — they called it a refrigerator — that kept food from spoiling!

I was speechless. This America truly was a wonderland!

AUGUST–
DECEMBER 1939
LEARNING TO BE
AN AMERICAN

*H*ans had a small business, and I helped him for a few dollars and room and board. I visited many wholesale houses in downtown New York and learned to do the things New Yorkers do: push my way into overcrowded subway cars, eat lunch on the run, and chew gum. (Most importantly, chew gum. That, I thought, seemed to be the hallmark of a true American.)

And I learned the language. I knew some English, of course, but I didn't know American. I picked up a few expressions which, I was told, were not used in good company. And I went to the movies! Sometimes I sat through the same picture two or three times, my ears wide open, so I could catch the sound of the language.

One word I learned the hard way: I bought what I thought was a bottle of hair tonic. I took it home, read the instructions, wet my hair, poured the "tonic" on, and wound up with a head full of soap bubbles.

☆ ☆ ☆

One night I was jarred out of my sleep. The lights in the room were on, and the radio was blaring. The family stood around me, consternation and anxiety in their faces. The German Army had invaded Poland. It was the beginning of World War II.

I thanked God for having taken me out of Europe in the nick of time, and I begged him to help my parents and our many relatives who were left behind.

☆ ☆ ☆

A great number of the refugees who had come from Europe settled in the area where we lived — near the George Washington Bridge — and the natives were becoming a bit antagonistic. The Jewish Center in New York practically pleaded with us to "get out of New York." They offered to give us bus fare and a letter of recommendation to the Jewish Center anywhere in the United States — anywhere, no questions asked. I told them I would like to go to Hollywood. (Perhaps there my dream of becoming a movie director or actor would be fulfilled.)

"Fine," they said, "we can send you to Hollywood, but you'll have to wait three weeks until we have a bus going to California."

I asked, "Don't you have a bus leaving earlier?"

"Yes," they replied, "we have a bus leaving tomorrow, but it goes to Chicago."

Chicago sounded as good as any other place — I could always become a movie director later. So the next day I thanked Hans and Liesl for their wonderful hospitality, took my suitcase, and boarded the bus to Chicago.

EARLY 1940

THE ANNOYED RABBI

AND THE NOT-SO-

TRUTHFUL ELAINE

*T*he Jewish Center in Chicago was on North Wells Street. The people there were just as eager to help us penniless refugees as their counterparts in New York had been. I am eternally grateful to American Jews who had opened their hearts and their pocketbooks to give us a start in this new land. I often ask God to bless them.

The Center sent me to a German-Jewish refugee family on the northwest side. Since they had a large apartment, they took in several boarders. Needless to say, the Center paid my expenses and promised to find me my first job.

☆ ☆ ☆

Alone among strangers in a strange city, I began to feel the need for God. I needed something to give meaning to my life. There was a synagogue not far from where I lived, and I went there on Friday evening, eager to learn more about the God who had done so much for me.

The service began with prayers and some hymns. Then the rabbi, a very important-looking man, stepped up to the lectern and began the sermon. His topic was "Why the Democrats lost the election." I was a very green immigrant, knowing nothing about American politics, and whatever he said sailed right over my head. I left the synagogue with a feeling of utter emptiness.

But I went back the following Friday. This time he spoke on "My trip to Florida." At one point he said, "My trip could have been very enjoyable; what spoiled it were *the many refugees* there." Needless to say, *this* refugee did not go back to hear him again.

Was I angry at the rabbi? No, I felt sorry for him. I pitied him for his narrow-mindedness and self-complacency.

☆ ☆ ☆

One evening a friend invited me to a club for German immigrants called The New Home Club. He said, "You will enjoy it. There will be entertainment." The "entertainment" turned out to be a heated discussion between club members trying to decide how to best use the club's finances: Should they rescue European Jews from Hitler or send their children to a summer camp? There was no agreement in sight. Finally, the president spoke up, "Before we reach any decision, let us find out how much money we have at our disposal. Will the treasurer please give his report." The man arose, looked at his papers, cleared his throat, and said, "At present we have a total of ten dollars and seventeen cents."

A young lady sat near me. We looked at each other and burst out laughing. That's how I met Elaine (not her real name). She was an American who had somehow wandered into this immigrants' meeting. She had unusual charm and impressed me very much. She was taking courses at a nearby university. She often carried a stack of books in her arms and seemed to know many important and educated people.

But then I found out that Elaine had to be taken with the proverbial grain of salt. We had a rendezvous one evening. I saw her coming across the street. Just then *her brother* approached her. I recognized him instantly; we had met for a moment at their home. They stopped and talked for a minute; then he walked on. When I came near her, she said, "That fellow asked me for a date many times, but I'm not interested."

Too bad for Elaine! She had forgotten that I had previously met her brother.

1940-1941

GOD, MY MOTHER,

AND I

*O*n early spring, the Jewish Center called. They had a job for me. It was a long, long step away from what I hoped to be: an actor or movie director. I was hired as a *busboy* at a country club in the village of Idlewild, Illinois. It wasn't much, but I didn't mind it. I received room and board and ten dollars a week, and I loved living in the country.

One evening I strolled down to the little village. I glanced at the newsstand in front of the drugstore, and my blood ran cold. The headline read, "German troops occupy Paris."

"Dear God," I said, "how long before Hitler will have all of Europe? Will I be able to save my mother from the death camps? Will it be too late?"

The summer passed; at the onset of cold weather, the club closed and I had to find another job. One of the club's members, Mr. Gimbel, owned an elegant restaurant on Randolph Street in Chicago. I went to see him, and he hired me on the spot.

☆ ☆ ☆

Now that I lived in Chicago, I had to see what I could do for my mother. A small agency I contacted said it could get passage for her on a Portuguese liner. The price was two hundred dollars. *Dear God, it might as well have been two thousand!* I had ten dollars to my name. What could I do?

A fellow worker had some advice. "Go to the X Bible Institute. They help people who need money." I phoned and got an appointment at seven o'clock one morning.

The man was impersonal; his face expressionless. He listened to me. Then he said, "I am sorry, we have no funds for this type of situation." When he saw my disappointment, he added, "If you could accept Jesus Christ as your Savior, you would have peace in your heart and you could be reconciled to your mother's death."

I exploded, "I don't want to be reconciled to her death. I want to save her life!"

He shook his head, "That's the trouble with the Jews. They won't listen."

There was only one thing I could do: I borrowed from everybody I could think of — twenty dollars here, fifteen dollars there — and I kept a list of all my lenders so I could eventually repay them.

When I had the two hundred dollars scraped together, I went to the agency, only to find out that the price had gone up to two hundred and fifty dollars. I borrowed some more, but when I came back the cost of the ticket was now three hundred dollars. From there it climbed to three hundred and fifty and then to four hundred dollars. "You know, Mr. Waldmann, these are uncertain times. We have to bribe people at every border and at every port."

I was ashamed to go back to my lenders and ask for more, but what else could I do? At last, I had every bit I needed and

I took it to the agency. This, I hoped, would be the final amount.

But a few days later I received the *bad* news: "Mr. Waldmann, the ship will not travel. It's too dangerous. Too many mines in the Atlantic."

I said, "Well, give me my money back."

"We can't do that right now, Mr. Waldmann. We sent your money to the main office in New York, but we can write to them and ask them to return it."

A suspicion crept into my head: "What if they'd tell me that the office in New York had sent my money to Portugal?" I was not about to wait and find out! I borrowed another twenty dollars, left a note for my boss, and took the first train to New York.

☆ ☆ ☆

I arrived at seven o'clock in the morning. My cousin Hans helped me find the agency. There I spoke to the president, and a short while later, had my check for four hundred dollars.

It was ten o'clock on Sunday evening when I came back to Chicago; in my pocket was the check and *twenty-five cents* in cash. I was almost starved. I debated whether to buy something for dinner or save the quarter for breakfast. I decided on breakfast, so I drank a glass of water and went to bed. The next morning I splurged the twenty-five cents on a roll and a cup of coffee. (Remember, the year was 1941.)

I cashed the check and repaid all my lenders. My heart was heavy. I had tried my utmost but had failed. I knew my mother's life would end in one of the death camps. But there was nothing I could do — nothing whatsoever.

☆ ☆ ☆

Then the unbelievable happened: One evening a telegram arrived. I thought to myself, "Oh, God! It's all over! What can

I do?" I opened it. It was from my mother, and it was from Spain. SPAIN? How did she get to Spain? It read, "Arrived Barcelona. Next stop New York."

How did it happen? How was this possible?

She had been summoned to Gestapo headquarters. The SS man told her, "You have one month to get out of Austria. If not, you'll be shipped to a concentration camp."

She pleaded for more time. "My son is in America. He is trying very hard to get me passage to America. Here is his latest telegram." And she placed it on his desk.

He brushed the telegram off the desk and shouted, "One month! Or I'll personally see to it that you are shipped off! I would even put you on a special train!"

She went home, saying, "I have connections at the Gestapo. They offered me a private train." It was gallows humor, a desperate attempt to keep her equilibrium in the face of impending disaster.

The next day she was at the Jewish Center, begging for help. But the answer was the same as she had heard dozens of times before, "There is nothing we can do. It's wartime. There are no ships crossing the Atlantic."

It was late afternoon, and the staff had left. But she kept walking through the empty corridors, hoping for something to turn up.

She passed the open door of an office. There were two men inside. One of them called out, "It's Mrs. Waldmann. We *have* to do something for her. Her son has tried so hard to help her." He called her in and told her they would get passage for her on a freighter, one of the last ships to cross the Atlantic.

Thus she traveled, together with a handful of other refugees, sleeping on deck, exposed to the elements, with rats and mice running over them.

Again her unique sense of humor sustained her. She said to her fellow travelers, "I don't like the accommodations on this ship. I'm getting off at the next stop." The next stop, of course, was America.

(Sometime later, I heard through a third person that there was a little woman aboard this ship who had everybody in stitches. No doubt, it was my mother.)

☆ ☆ ☆

It was late August when, with an eager heart, I walked into the railroad terminal in Chicago. As the train pulled in and the mass of people emerged, I spotted her, my little old mother whom I had given up for dead.

And when I held her in my arms, I could only thank God who had made the impossible possible.

☆ ☆ ☆

DISCERNING THE WILL OF GOD

☆ ☆ ☆

EARLY 1942

THE CHOSEN PEOPLE?

*I*t was January 1942, and the restaurant began to pall on me. I certainly didn't want to spend the rest of my life as a busboy.

I went to the Jewish Center to see if their people could help me find a different job. They gave me an aptitude test; one of the questions surprised me: "If you were free to choose any occupation, what would you like to be?" My answer: "A movie director." The young lady made a quick phone call and then handed me a slip of paper with an address. It wasn't a movie studio; it was the clothing workers' union.

The man there asked, "You're a tailor?"

"No, I'm not a tailor, but I have experience in…"

"You want to learn to be a tailor?"

"Yes, I would like to learn to…"

He picked up the phone. "What kind of people are you sending me? What can I do with him? I can only send him to Alfred Decker and Cohn."

This, I said to myself, must be the worst dump in the city of Chicago. I was wrong. It was a twelve-story building full of professionals, and — as I soon found out — the clothing they manufactured was a high-quality product.

They took me to the sixth floor, gave me a stack of half-finished coats, and told me to trim off the excess material. "Not too much but not too little, and don't cut too close to the edge or you'll ruin the coat." I'm slow by nature, and I worked even more slowly for fear of ruining the coats. It was piecework, and I just about earned the minimum wage.

One day the foreman took me to a sewing machine, gave me a hasty ten-minute instruction, and then left me to struggle on my own. And struggle I did. It was clear I had no talent for tailoring, and in no time I was back at my first job, trimming coats. Again I had come to a dead end in my life. I had to get out of that place!

But little did I know that in this very place, my life was just beginning.

☆ ☆ ☆

Across the aisle from where I worked sat a very plain, very mousy girl. She began to talk to me, and one day she said in her monotone, "If you would go out with me, you wouldn't have to spend a lot of money." I wasn't interested. I couldn't picture myself spending an evening in her company.

Once, while barely listening to the mousy girl across the aisle, I let my eyes wander about the vast room. In the distance I spotted a lovely face with a radiant smile — a smile that broke through the sea of dull expressions the way a sudden sunbeam breaks through a gray sky.

I asked the talkative girl, "Who is *that?*"

"Oh, that's Florence."

"She is...I mean, is she married?"

"Oh, no, Florence isn't married."

From that moment on, I spent every spare minute hanging around Florence. She was a delightful person with a charming face. Her whole being seemed to radiate an inner joy which I had never seen in anybody. Intelligent and mature, she was great fun to be with. Without a trace of affectation or pretense about her, she was truly genuine.

Wanting to get to know her better, I asked her for a date — maybe a movie on Saturday? I got a warm smile and a firm "No." I persisted. "What about Sunday?" Same reply. I tried again the following week and the week after that. Finally, she explained, she didn't go out often; she spent much of her time in church.

Now *that* I couldn't understand at all! I had seen churches in Vienna: Saint Stephen's Cathedral, which I regularly passed on my way to work, and Saint John Nepomuk in our neighborhood. Of course, I never entered either of them; but I glanced through the open doors as I passed by, and they looked gloomy, gloomy, gloomy. How could a vivacious person like Florence spend her time in a gloomy place like a church?

It was early spring when for the first time we left work together and walked down Michigan Avenue. We found we had a million things to talk about. After that, we spent some happy, fun-filled Sundays together, and I *knew* that I had found the person with whom I would like to spend the rest of my life.

Imagine my shock when one day she announced she may have to stop seeing me. "Why, for heaven's sake? Why?" She had a friend, she explained — sort of an adviser — who told her it wouldn't be wise to keep company with a young man of another religion.

I flew off the handle, "I'd like to see the guy who says you shouldn't go out with me!"

She asked quietly, "Would you *really* like to see him?"

"Yes, I would!"

"You know, he is a priest."

"A pr...a priest? Yes, sure, makes no difference."

☆ ☆ ☆

One afternoon Florence and I took the streetcar to Notre Dame Church on Harrison Street. We rang the bell at the church rectory and a smiling man in a black cassock showed us to a parlor. Through the open door, I saw some other black-robed figures. I had the eerie feeling that I was going to my own funeral. Another man in a black robe put his head through the door, waved "hello" to Florence, and smilingly asked me, "What are *you* doing here with this dangerous woman?"

That's all I needed! The place felt creepy enough, but this "dangerous woman" bit threw me into a tizzy. What were they up to? Maybe they would pour holy water over me and try to make me a Catholic by force! I looked around the room; it was on the first floor. I thought if they would get rough, I could easily jump out the window.

Just then Florence's priest-friend entered. He was short — maybe a little over five feet. His name was Father Boissoneault. So *this* was the man who had advised Florence not to go out with me anymore! I was ready to take him on.

We shook hands and sat down. Florence mentioned she had bought new shoes and a bag to match, and he commended her good taste. Then for a few minutes they discussed the high prices of merchandise. I expected a priest to talk about religion. "Maybe," I thought to myself, "he *had* no religion."

I can't remember how the topic of the conversation

90

changed, but all of a sudden, he said, "The Jews are the Chosen People of God."

That got my goat! I had heard that expression all my life, and I always thought it showed a lot of arrogance on our part.

I snapped at him, "I'd like to know *who* said we're the Chosen People!"

He smiled, "God said it."

I opened my mouth and forgot to close it. And he sat there, shaking with laughter.

I left the place even more bewildered than when I had arrived.

SUMMER 1942
ABOUT ABRAHAM AND
OTHER JEWS

*O*ne afternoon Florence and I walked by a church, and she asked if I would mind coming in and waiting while she said some prayers. It was a small, intimate-looking church. The sun shone through the stained-glass windows that gave it a homey look. I picked up a prayer book and opened it at random: "May the God of Abraham, the God of Isaac, the God of Jacob, be with you, and may he fulfill in you his blessing...." What was I reading? Was this a Jewish prayer book? Was I in a synagogue? I was completely disoriented. What was Abraham doing in a Christian prayer book?

I asked Florence for an explanation. She said, "That shouldn't surprise you. Jesus was a Jew."

Now *that* really amazed me! Not that she *knew* Jesus was a Jew — everybody knows that — but that Catholics have the courage to admit it!

☆ ☆ ☆

We went back to see Father Boissoneault once in a while. I really liked the little man. He never tried to persuade me. If I had a question, he answered it briefly — sometimes too briefly. Once I said to him, "I wonder what it is that gives Florence this joyous disposition? And why do I feel such *inner peace* when I'm in her company?"

He replied, "It's the presence of God in her." What did he mean by that?

Once he told me about two Jews who had become Catholics. One had been a socialist lecturer; now he lectured on the Catholic faith. The other case was even stranger: This one had been a sailor — a Jewish sailor! — who had become a priest! Unbelievable!

☆ ☆ ☆

The ex-socialist lecturer had written some books about the Catholic religion, and Florence brought me one of them. She thought it might answer the many questions bouncing around in my head. She was wrong. In this book he made some strange statements, for example: Jesus was the Messiah promised to the Jewish people long ago, and he was *divine.*

Well, I sat down and wrote to this man. His name was David Goldstein. I asked him, "If the Catholic Church is so good, why is it that at the beginning of World War I the Catholic priests in Austria blessed the weapons of war?" (I read that in the socialist press.)

His answer was ridiculous. "I don't know why the priests in Austria blessed the weapons of war; presumably so they would bring about peace. But this has no bearing on whether or not you should become a Catholic."

I yelled, "The guy is out of his mind! Who wants to become a Catholic?"

☆ ☆ ☆

Something very strange happened one Saturday afternoon. I was at Florence's house, and the phone rang. I said to myself, "This call is for me." But just as quickly, I dismissed the thought. I had never given Florence's phone number to anyone.

Florence answered the call. She said, "Kurt? Yes, he is right here." The call *was* for me.

It was Father Klyber, the Jewish priest. He explained that Goldstein had written to him about me. He asked if we would like to visit him in suburban Glenview. I said, "The Jewish priest? Yes, definitely! *This* oddity I have to see!"

On Sunday afternoon, Florence and I took the Milwaukee Avenue bus to the end of the line. In a car waiting for us was Father Klyber. He stepped out, and I saw he wore a long, black cassock. I felt very embarrassed. What if somebody would see me in the company of a priest?

He led us into the monastery and opened the door to a parlor. At that moment I had an eerie experience: On a table I saw a small, black book with red edges. At the sight of it, I recoiled. I strongly felt that this book contained the essence of evil....

Father Klyber said that he heard I had some questions. I certainly did! But I had not come for explanations; I had come to argue. The idea that this Jew was a priest was too much! I fired away at him, but for every answer he tried to give me, I had a "Yes but" or a "How come?" He finally threw up his hands: "This will lead you nowhere. You should take a regular course of instructions and all your questions will be answered in due time."

"Ha!" I said to myself, "No course of instructions for me! At the end of it, he'll probably tell me I'm ready to be baptized!"

When we left, he gave me a few pamphlets he had written and invited us to come and see him again. He was a likable

94

fellow, this Father Klyber. I wondered how he, as a Jew, could feel at home in this strange environment.

I read the pamphlets. They all said the same thing: Jesus was the Messiah, and he had come to give us eternal life. This all sounded very nice, but it meant nothing to me.

DECEMBER 4, 1942
THE DEMISE OF IF

*W*ere there ever two people more delighted to be with each other than Florence and I? Yet when we spoke of marriage, it was always with a big IF. There were too many seemingly insurmountable obstacles.

But then came December 4, 1942, and IF never saw the light of day again. It was an ordinary weekday. Florence and I left work together, climbed the stairs to the el station, and sat shivering on the icy platform, waiting for the train. Neither of us can remember the exact words we spoke, but at that moment we understood that we had been born for each other, that we belonged to each other, that IF could have no part in our lives, that neither of us would ever want to exist without the other again.

To this day we celebrate December 4 as the day when we really found each other. To this day we call December 4 "Our Day."

1943

I DON'T PLAY GAMES

WITH GOD

*C*icero, the well-known Chicago suburb, was home to many machine shops. It was in one of these that I found my next job.

I loved working with metal. As much as I had felt out of place in the tailor shop, here I was perfectly at home. I loved the precision inherent in this work, the absolute accuracy demanded in every step of a project. I learned to read blueprints and to operate complicated machinery.

I stayed ten years in this job. They became the most eventful ten years of my life.

☆ ☆ ☆

I am fortified — or should I say "afflicted" — with a very suspicious nature. Before I can believe anything, I have to investigate it to the nth degree. So it was with the Catholic Church. I had the notion that everything I was told, everything I was given to read, was slanted to lure me into the Church. In a calm moment, however, I had to admit that this was probably nonsense. Florence never talked about her religion, the two priests I knew only answered my questions, and the books I read were not written *for me*. But the suspicion remained; I stayed constantly on the watch not to be taken in.

But just when I thought I had all my defenses in place, a startling question popped into my mind: We are *all* God's children, Jew and Gentile alike. Wouldn't God want *all* of us to follow him in *one* religion? Could it perhaps be that the Catholic Church *is* that religion? Could it be that Jesus Christ really *is* God?

My first reaction was to banish it from my mind, to dismiss it as something I shouldn't even think about. But it kept coming back. Was God trying to tell me something? If I ignored the whole thing, would I be *ignoring God?*

There was only one thing to do: I had to investigate. I had to ask more questions, read more books, and examine every claim until I would arrive at the definite answer: Yes or No. But there was a problem with that. The more I read, the more I heard, the more confused and undecided I became. But that did not deter me; I was determined to get to the truth. Sometimes this search took on ridiculous proportions. In one of his books, David Goldstein stated that any Catholic with a clear conscience could say the well-known Jewish prayer, "Hear, O Israel, the Lord, our God, is One." (By this he wanted to show the relationship between the Jewish and Catholic religions.) I wondered whether Goldstein knew Hebrew well enough to get the *true* meaning of the prayer? Could I perhaps study Hebrew to find out?...

Another question began to nag me: No doubt, all these Catholics were very sincere, but what if they were *mistaken?* On the other hand, their Scriptures are full of examples that Christ performed deeds that no mere human can perform: Lazarus had been dead for four days — his body was decaying — and Christ restored him to life. The blind young man — sightless since birth — was given sight....

It was enough to drive me crazy. I couldn't accept all this on hearsay. *I had to be sure.*

Father Klyber had a suggestion, "Pray. Speak to God in your own words. Ask him to lead you. He *cannot* mislead you." And then, somewhat absent-mindedly, he added, "Some day you will be a Catholic. And it won't be because of what I say or what anybody else says. Some day, on your own, you will become a Catholic." Silly, wasn't he?

But I did pray. For weeks on end, when I walked the streets, when I rode the streetcar, I pleaded with God, "Please, show me what you want me to do. I want to do your will." But he remained silent.

Then one day I decided to force his hand. It was a Saturday. I said to God, "Tomorrow I will go to a Catholic church to pray. If you don't want me to go there, please make me so sick that I can't leave the house. But just for this one day. Make me well again on Monday. I must go to work; I must earn money." (Was this too much to ask of God? Is he not omnipotent?)

Sunday came and I was in perfect health. After lunch I took the bus to St. Mel's Church on Washington Boulevard. I walked up the ten or twelve steps, cautiously opened the door, and looked inside. The large vestibule was empty. I could feel the tension in my body as I opened the door to the church. It was large, sun-filled, and empty. I took a few steps inside and sat down in the last pew. Then I said, "God, I'm here!" Nothing. I added, "I'm here to *pray!*" Still nothing. Dead silence. I waited a few seconds; then I jumped up and hurried out.

The sun shone as I walked west on Washington Boulevard. I had not noticed it before. My heart had been too full of anxiety. I said to myself, "I had gone into a Catholic church to speak to God, and he had not stopped me. But what did it *really* mean? What was he trying to tell me?"

I told Florence about my venture. She looked at me and said

very quietly, "If you would become a Catholic only to please me, I would not marry you." I was truly astonished. Did she know me so little? I replied, "You don't have to worry. I will be what God wants me to be. I don't play games with God."

☆ ☆ ☆

Thanksgiving Day came and I went to see Florence early in the afternoon. We took the bus downtown. As we walked along Dearborn Street, she suggested, "Why don't we start the day by going to church to ask for God's blessing?"

Old St. Peter's Church was nearby. As we came out, I spotted a pamphlet rack in the vestibule. One of the pamphlets caught my eye. Its title was *I Wish I Could Believe.* I read it as we walked down the street. It explained that faith in Christ is a personal gift of God. We cannot receive it by reasoning or by studying. Even an angel from heaven could not give it. Only God himself can bestow it.

It was a warm, sunny day, and I felt warm and sunny inside. I had the distinct feeling that things would work out for Florence and me, that we would have a wonderful life together — she as a Catholic and I as a Jew.

☆ ☆ ☆

But the next day all hell broke loose. At work I kept making mistakes. The more I tried to concentrate, the worse it got. The superintendent came by and attempted to help me. That only increased my nervousness.

Suddenly, I had an eerie experience. I saw before me, as on a large movie screen, the interior of St. Thomas Aquinas Church. I saw several people in the center aisle genuflecting before the altar. Then all at once their movements changed, and they jumped up and down like big apes. An intense feeling of disgust for anything Catholic came over me.

I was still struggling with my work. The superintendent came back and, without a word, looked over my shoulder. This put me into a state of near panic. At this very instant a thought pushed itself into my tortured brain, *They say there is a Devil, but there is no Devil. They only use this to scare little children.* I considered this for a split second and agreed. Then it hurriedly continued, *If they can say there is a Devil — and there is no Devil — they can also say, "There is a God, and there is no God."*

"Stop! Stop!" I almost shouted it! Instantly the picture vanished, the suggestions ceased, and my work proceeded without a hitch.

☆ ☆ ☆

In the days that followed, I felt an ever-growing revulsion for anything Catholic. It was as if I had never admired Catholics for their sincerity, their strength of conviction. From day to day, there grew in me the feeling that, contrary to anything I had ever seen, these Catholics were a ridiculous, superstitious sect. And at the same time, I developed a distaste for my Jewish religion.

I was indescribably miserable during these days. I tried to pull myself together and reason this whole thing out, but it was no use. I was mentally, physically, and emotionally drained — an absolute wreck.

THE INFINITE

DECEMBER 2, 1943

OF COURSE,

CHRIST IS GOD

A week had gone by since that Thanksgiving Day when I saw a happy future for Florence and myself. I wasn't the same person anymore. In all honesty, I had to tell Florence what she could expect of life with me. We met at a coffee shop at the corner of Cicero and Washington. I told her in plain words, "I'm through with religion — *any* religion — Catholic, Jewish, any…I don't want to talk about it anymore, I don't want to think about it anymore. If you still want to marry me, I won't interfere with your religion. If we have children, they can be baptized Catholic."

After that, there wasn't much to say. Florence quietly asked if I would walk a couple of blocks with her. She wanted to make a visit at church.

I said, "Sure. Let's cross over to the other side of the street."

She looked surprised, "Why cross over? The church is on *this* side."

I replied, "I don't even want to walk on the same sidewalk where there is a Catholic church."

It is to Florence's credit that she recognized my disturbed state of mind and gave in to my senseless request. She followed me to the other side, and we walked the two blocks in near silence. When we reached the point opposite the church, I did something which is against every one of my principles. I let her dash across the street by herself — amid the heavy traffic. I felt like an idiot standing there and watching her, but I wouldn't get near that church — for anything.

I took the next bus home. My mother remarked, "You look very tired. After supper you should take your bath and go to bed early." That's all I wanted.

While eating, I read the comics in the newspaper. No more deep studies for me, no more searching, no more...

I finished my meal, walked into the bathroom, and began preparation for shaving. (I shaved in the evening because I had to get up very early, but then I went to work with stubble on my face.)

I remember distinctly that my mind was an absolute void. I thought of nothing but a warm bath and a good night's sleep — nothing else. What happened the next instant is almost impossible to describe in human language. But I will try to tell it as well and as accurately as I can.

A thought entered my mind. I use the term *entered* because it was not my own thought. It came peacefully, slowly, and very distinctly, as if someone placed the words before me — one at a time. It was unmistakable. It said, "Of course, Christ is God. How could you ever doubt it?"

Nonplussed, I looked at myself in the bathroom mirror and said, "Yes, how *could* I ever doubt it?" At that moment I not only believed that Christ is God, I knew it. I knew it as clearly as I know that I am Kurt Waldmann. Dumbfounded, I said, "I must have known it all my life. I must have just forgotten it."

I sat down on the edge of the bathtub. Undoubtedly, this was the gift of Faith I had read about. I smiled to myself, "Wonderful! I'm a Catholic!" But then the old suspicious Kurt came to the fore. "Just a moment now! You know practically nothing about the Catholic Church." But I quickly answered myself, "Yes, but didn't I always say if I believed that Christ is God, I'd accept everything his Church teaches?"

I washed the shaving cream off my face and walked into the living room. Not tired anymore, I was filled with a peace and lightheartedness I had never known before. I saw my mother resting on the couch, and I begged God to give her the same blessing he had given me. There was a radio on a small table near the window. A male voice sang the then-popular song, "Yours Is My Heart Alone." I sat down on the carpet in front of the radio, and in my heart I sang that song to Jesus Christ, my Adonai and my God, "Yours is my heart alone." My mother asked, "What's the matter with you? Have you gone crazy? Why do you sit on the floor?"

When I closed my eyes that night, I knew I had become a new person. From now on, I would live my life for my Messiah, who had invited me to be one of his own.

WINTER 1943-44
IT'S MATZA!

*M*orning came and I went to work. I wondered whether the other workers would notice the change that had taken place in me. They all went about their usual tasks, cracked their usual jokes, and lived for the moment when the bell would ring and they could storm out of the place. I was an island of happiness in a humdrum world.

I counted the minutes until I could share my joy with Florence. It was Friday, and I knew she would be at evening services — at the very church I had refused to come near the evening before. This time I entered, blessed myself with holy water, and genuflected. There were only a few people left — services must have been over for a while. From the semidarkness, I heard Florence's footsteps. I rose, genuflected, and blessed myself again. Florence didn't notice.

Outside, I eagerly started, "Can you stand some good news?"

She gave me a weary look, "I *sure* can!" It came from the depth of her tired soul. It sounded like a cry for help.

I quickly continued, "Remember, Father Klyber once said I would become a Catholic on my own...."

"Yes. What about it?"

I shouted, "It happened! It happened!"

There was a touch of impatience in her look and in her voice, "Whaaat happened?"

My joy bubbled over. Laughter just poured out of me. I was so full of happiness — and poor little Florence looked so bewildered! Unable to speak, I held on to a lamppost and just laughed and laughed....

At last, after catching my breath, I explained to her in minute detail what had occurred the night before. And slowly, ever so slowly, she began to understand that I had been given the most precious of all gifts, the gift of Faith.

☆ ☆ ☆

Now I hastened to tell our two priest-friends. Father Boissoneault listened to me in silence, his penetrating eyes fastened on me. He did not interrupt; he asked no questions. When I had finished, I saw tears in his eyes.

Father Klyber had one question, "Did you hear a voice?" When I said "No," he nodded his approval. Obviously, he was satisfied that my experience had been genuine. Then he said, "Now that you believe, I want to show you something." He took me into a small room behind the altar. There he opened a cabinet, took out a metal container, and from it he took a thin, round wafer and said, "Eat it."

I hesitated. I had a feeling it was something sacred.

He urged, "Go ahead, eat it. It's not consecrated."

I ate it, and in surprise I cried out, "It's matza!"

☆ ☆ ☆

Father Klyber and I began the series of instructions he had suggested long ago. During the following weeks, I learned what Christ's Church teaches and *why* she teaches it.

Imagine my happy surprise when I found that the Catholic

Church calls Abraham "our father in faith." Imagine my joy when I read in Catholic Scripture that "salvation is from the Jews" (John 4:22).

For the first time in my life, I understood why we are called the "Chosen People." It was from *our* people that the Savior of the world was to come. It was from our people that he chose his apostles: Simon, surnamed Peter, Saul, called Paul, Levi, called Matthew, Nathaniel, and the rest of the Twelve. I was overjoyed when I realized that thousands upon thousands of Jews before me had given their allegiance to Christ.

All my life I had carried my Jewishness like a burden — an object of ridicule and hatred. How often I had wished that I could blend into the crowd!

Not anymore! Today, I thank God for the privilege he has given me — the privilege of being a Jew!

☆ ☆ ☆

On February 27, 1944, Father Klyber received me into the Catholic Church. I chose "Paul" as my baptismal name, in honor of that great Jew, Saul of Tarsus, commonly known as Saint Paul. I chose him as my patron since he — and I — intensely hated the Church of Christ and since he — and I — were given to see the Truth, in a flash, in the "twinkling of an eye."

MAY–JULY 1945

MARRIED LIFE ON

A ROLLER COASTER

*I*t was early May, and the persistent obstacles to our upcoming marriage suddenly disappeared like a puff of smoke. We hastened to inform Father Boissoneault, and the wedding was set for May 12.

During these days, the weather in Chicago was dismal. Heavy rain on our wedding day was a distinct possibility. I begged God, practically every minute, not to let our day be spoiled — and something remarkable happened: Each time I whispered a prayer, the sun broke through the gray clouds for a couple of seconds and then hid again. It was as if God reassured me, "Don't worry. It will be all right."

May 12 came and the earth was bathed in brilliant sunshine. We pronounced our vows at Notre Dame Church, in the presence of Father Boissoneault. The impossible dream had become reality.

We spent a delightful week at an unusually pleasant hotel on the near north side, rejoicing in the knowledge that now we were really one.

☆ ☆ ☆

But we had an immediate problem: We had to find a place to live. There were no vacant apartments anywhere, so we decided on a rooming house as a temporary solution. It turned out to be a lot more temporary than anticipated. We moved in one afternoon and moved out the next morning. We spent the night fully dressed, dodging the cockroaches.

Back to a hotel we went, this time a rather expensive place near Michigan Avenue. We lived in a large, beautiful room, ate at only good restaurants, and watched our small savings disappear.

☆ ☆ ☆

On June 26, Florence and I went to the U.S. District Court in Chicago where, as one in a large group of aliens, I renounced my allegiance to my native country and swore allegiance to the United States of America. It was one of the happiest moments of my life. I was proud to be called a citizen of the country which had opened its arms to me when my life had been in mortal danger.

At the same time, I officially changed my name from Kurt to Paul, the name I had taken in baptism. It was, to me, another pledge of allegiance — allegiance to my Messiah.

☆ ☆ ☆

Our savings depleted, we had to get a place less expensive than the hotel. Fortunately, we found a very clean room at the home of a pleasant widow. It looked like the end of trouble, but it was really the beginning of near disaster.

The day we moved I had to transport — *lug* is a better word — our belongings from one place to the other by streetcar from early morning until afternoon. I became overheated, caught a sudden chill, and the result, in the doctor's words, was "a touch of tuberculosis."

I had great difficulty breathing, could not raise my voice above a whisper, and was unbelievably weak. Work, of course, was out.

Our "pleasant" landlady concluded that I was "one of those fellows who sits around all day and lets his wife support him."

But I was not disheartened. I said, "If God gave this, it must be good." This also aroused criticism. A friend told me, "That is *not* the way to pray. You must ask God to *help* you." But I preferred to trust divine Providence.

The doctor sent me to a tuberculosis clinic. There I was

examined, x-rayed, and told to return in a couple of weeks for "collapse therapy." I had no idea what that was.

One evening Florence and I were at services at Our Lady of Sorrows Church. The congregation sang, but I could only whisper the words of the hymn. Singing was impossible. There wasn't enough breath in my diseased lungs. But suddenly — I don't know how — my full voice was back, loud and clear. Astonished, I looked at Florence. She raised her head toward me; there were tears in her eyes.

A few days later I went back to the clinic. The doctor took another x-ray, examined it, and called in two other doctors. The three scrutinized the film for a long time and finally said, "There is no sign of illness in your lungs. You are cured."

☆ ☆ ☆

Another wonderful thing happened: We found an apartment. We bought furniture and moved in on July 19. Two days later we went to get my mother, who had been living alone since the day of our wedding. We packed her belongings and brought her to our home.

She seemed quite content. The language barrier between her and Florence wasn't too much of a problem; Florence tried to learn some German, and my mother had picked up a few words of English. And, of course, I was there as an interpreter. All was harmony.

☆ ☆ ☆

On July 27, Florence and I came home from work. It was only six days since my mother had moved in with us. It was Friday evening. My mother had Sabbath candles burning, and she told us laughingly that she had listened to a German language radio broadcast, had danced a waltz by herself, and had a good laugh.

I asked, "Why? Was the program so funny?"

She replied, "On the contrary, the announcer said it would be a comedy, but there wasn't a single good joke in it. I thought it was hilarious!"

She had that rare sense of humor, that gift to see the ridiculous in any situation and laugh at it.

☆ ☆ ☆

It had been a stifling hot day in Chicago, and evening brought no relief. We moved my mother's bed to the window so she could get a breath of air. (Remember, it was 1945. No air conditioning.)

At three in the morning, she knocked at our bedroom door. "Please, help me. I'm sick." I led her back to her bed. She asked for her medicine, her nitroglycerin.

I rushed to get the medicine, but it was too late. She couldn't take it anymore. She managed to say, "This is the end."

I protested. "Don't say that! We'll take you to a hospital...."

She shook her head, "It's no use. It's the end. I know it." A minute later she said, "Hold me up. I can't breathe."

I put my arm under her shoulder and held her until she died. At that moment I *understood,* not only with the eyes of faith but in my mind as well, that there has to be life after death. It was inconceivable that this God-given keen intellect had suddenly ceased to exist.

There was great sadness but also great peace in my soul. My mother's difficult life on earth had ended; she had gone to spend a happy eternity with her God.

1946

GOD'S LITTLE GIRL

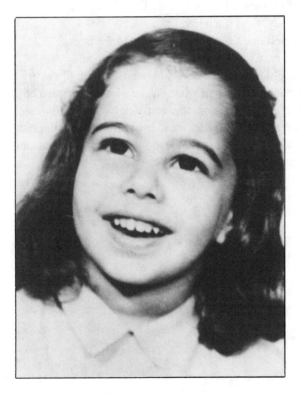

$\mathcal{T}$he day was October 5, 1946. Religious Jews spent the day in prayer and fasting. It was Yom Kippur, the Day of Atonement.

Since early morning, I had been at the maternity ward of St. Elizabeth Hospital. I don't know how long I had to wait — an hour, perhaps two. At last a door opened, and there on a stretcher was Florence. With a happy smile, she whispered, "We have a beautiful little girl."

We named her Mary Therese. She was a bright, happy, fun-loving child who enjoyed her simple games, but there were rare moments when her mother and I wondered what hidden knowledge this child had. How many four-year-olds ask you to read to them a book on Catholic spirituality?

"Daddy, read the book."

"Which one? *Goldilocks* or *The Three Bears*?"

"No, read the book you read to Mommy."

There she sat, her eyes wide open, drinking in every word.

Or take the moment when she and I walked into a church at the start of Benediction. She anxiously whispered to me, "Say the prayer!" And as the priest held high the monstrance with the sacred host, Mary Therese bowed in adoration until her forehead touched the floor.

1950
THE DISAPPEARANCE
OF THE HAM

*F*lorence's cousin Rosemarie came one evening and told us about an amateur theater group that was holding auditions for a play. She thought I should give it a try. The director, a professional, asked me to read a scene in which a traveling salesman speaks to the desk clerk at a hotel and is distracted by two girls walking through the lobby. I guess I improvised the scene very convincingly. I got a round of applause from the assembled thespians, and I got the part.

We held rehearsals but little by little several members of the group dropped out until we didn't have enough people left to give the performance. On our last evening together, our director sat down with the remaining five or six of us and gave each of us an evaluation. When she came to me, she said, "Waldmann is the born character actor. You give him any character part, and he'll play it."

This was the shot in the arm I needed. This professional's testimony was living proof that I was not beating the air; that I had the potential to make a name for myself in the theater.

115

An opportunity came only a few days later. The New Home Club planned a variety show, and they asked me to be their master of ceremonies. Of course, this wasn't theater in the true sense of the word, but it would give me an opportunity to work before an audience, to perfect my skill.

The evening of the performance came and I entered the place, full of anticipation. But right from the start, I felt nothing but boredom. This was strange. I had been in shows of this type before and had always felt the thrill and excitement that goes with being a performer. But this time the endless succession of mediocre singers and unfunny comedians brought home to me the banality of it all. Suddenly, I saw show business in a different light. I thought, "Is this to be my future life? Am I to exist only for the moment when I can stand in the limelight and hear a few people clap their hands?"

When the last comedian was on stage and I heard him rattle off a string of warmed-over jokes, I could bear it no longer. I had to get out. Behind the stage, there was a door that led to a small platform outside the building. I opened the door and stepped out. I was in almost complete darkness. Far below me was the deserted city street; above me the vast sky. The stars looked so close, it seemed I could almost touch them. There was total silence. I was alone with God.

I said to him, "Dear God, let me not waste my life on trivialities. Take from me this inane craving for applause, this running after other people's approval."

The show ended, and I was one of the first out of the place — never to set foot on a stage again. The ham was no more.

OCTOBER 1951–
MAY 1952
PEACE BEYOND
ALL UNDERSTANDING

*O*t was October 1951. Our daughter had just celebrated her fifth birthday in the company of her friends. Nothing whatsoever gave us an inkling that she would celebrate her *next* birthday in the presence of God and his angels.

She was a happy, healthy child, full of life and laughter. But one day we discovered a small lump under her chin. A month later she was in the hospital for removal of a small cyst. The subsequent biopsy revealed what we were afraid to even think: cancer.

My mind groped for an explanation. I remembered Abraham; how God had put him to the test by ordering him to sacrifice his only child. The similarity was striking. Surely this, too, was only a test! God wanted to see how willing we were to accept *his* will — and in the end, Mary Therese will be restored to perfect health.

The doctor ordered x-ray treatments, and by Christmas the

lump had disappeared. Mary Therese was again her happy self — but not for long. In February she was back in the hospital. The diagnosis: cancer of the tongue. A team of surgeons operated for four hours. A few days later we heard the dreadful verdict: It was one of the most rapid types of cancer; her condition was terminal.

☆ ☆ ☆

She came home and tried to do the things she had done before, but her movements were so much slower. She complained about her little girlfriend, "The trouble with Marilyn is that she is so fast."

Before long she lost all desire for food — a common occurrence with cancer patients, so doctors tell us — and she had to remain in bed. Big lumps appeared on her emaciated little body — especially on her back and head. And the cancerous mass began to fill her mouth.

By April her body resembled a skeleton. Her legs were bent at the knees, and the mere touch of a sheet caused her intense suffering. Yet she never uttered a word of complaint. One day, however, she broke into tears. Florence hurried to her side.

"Why are you crying?"

"I'm crying because Jesus suffered more than I."

What secret had God revealed to this little child?

☆ ☆ ☆

News of Mary Therese's illness had spread throughout the neighborhood. People's reactions ran the gamut.

The red-haired young Irish priest in our parish asked, "What's wrong with going to heaven when you're five, instead of seventy-five? You are saved seventy years of headaches."

Then there was the lady — a stranger — who stopped me on the street and asked, "Why should a thing like that happen to two nice people like you and your wife?"

I explained that Mary Therese would be living with God, that she would have eternal happiness, and that we would have our own saint in heaven.

She replied, "Yes, but why should this happen to you?"

☆ ☆ ☆

The day came when I could no longer go to work. I averaged one or two hours of sleep a night, and one morning the superintendent sent me home, "I'm afraid you're going to injure yourself. Come back when all this is over."

From then on, Florence and I spent our days and nights at Mary Therese's bedside, trying to give her what little comfort we could. The cancer now filled her entire mouth.

But we had *one* worry that outweighed all others: *how* she would die. The doctor mentioned two possibilities: Lack of food could literally starve her or the cancer in her mouth could suffocate her. We prayed — and asked everybody to help us pray — that she would have a peaceful death.

☆ ☆ ☆

Father Klyber phoned one day; he had come to Chicago and wanted to see us. We spent the evening in quiet conversation — only a few steps from Mary Therese's bed. She was asleep, her breathing barely noticeable. At one point we got up to look at her more closely. She had died.

Father blessed her. It was he who had received her into the Church at her baptism. God's providence had sent him back to her at the moment when she entered her eternity. The date was May 19, 1952. Mary Therese was five years and seven months old.

The funeral parlor overflowed. It seemed that every one of my fellow workers had come.

In her casket, our little girl looked like a shriveled old woman. The pretty young nun who had given her piano lessons

119

burst into tears at the sight of her pupil and had to be led out of the room. We asked a neighbor to bring Mary Therese's portrait from our house, so we could place it on the casket. We wanted everyone to see how very beautiful she had been.

On the day of the burial, a handful of relatives returned with us from the cemetery. We went through the motions of normal social behavior. We ate, we talked, but I dreaded the inevitable; the moment when our guests would leave and Florence and I would be left alone with our loss.

When we shut the door behind the last person, we looked at each other, and we both began to sob uncontrollably.

☆ ☆ ☆

Throughout the years, Irwin, one of my fellow workers, had taken great delight in needling me about my Faith. He thought it was just plain silly that I, a Jew, professed to be a Catholic. He was over six feet tall, looked straight down at me from his towering height, and tried his utmost to unsettle me.

It was a *different* Irwin who approached me on the day I returned to work after Mary Therese's funeral. He stood in front of me, watched my every move, and finally asked, "How do you *do* it?"

"How do I do what?"

"How do you go about your work as if nothing had happened — after what you have been through? How can you be so calm?"

I answered him in one word, "Faith."

☆ ☆ ☆

A year later I saw Irwin again. (I had left the firm and only returned for a visit.)

He said, "I have news for you."

"What's that?"

"I am taking instructions in the Catholic faith. I decided to become a Catholic."

"Would you...would you mind repeating that?"

"I am taking instructions in the Catholic faith. I decided to become a Catholic."

"What...I mean...what made you decide to do *that?*"

"I have a friend who has some emotional problems. I looked at him and said to myself, 'This poor fellow has nothing to hold on to.' And then I looked at myself and said, 'I have nothing to hold on to either.'"

He paused for a moment and then matter-of-factly added, "But what *really* made me decide was this: At your daughter's wake, you and your wife were the only ones smiling."

Lucky Irwin! He had discovered the peace beyond all understanding. (See Philippians 4:7.)

MAY 1952–MAY 1953
THE MOUNTAIN
OF THE LORD

*W*e had to start rebuilding our lives now. We needed something to fill the emptiness left in our hearts. First and foremost, we needed a different place to live. We had to get away from a situation which had been more than unpleasant for years.

Florence's cousin Jane was having a two-story house built, and she offered us the top-floor apartment. It was an elegant home on a street that was a credit to its name, Sunnyside Avenue.

We bought a rose-colored carpet for our twenty-foot living room; we were planning to get garden furniture for our large open-air porch; and I was considering an ornate mirror for our living-room wall. We could afford things now. Florence had begun to work at my firm; she was her usual excellent self and quickly caught the eye of top management. We had comfortably settled into a groove.

We didn't know we had a monumental surprise waiting for us. It was no less than an invitation from God.

☆ ☆ ☆

The phone rang one day; it was Father Klyber on the line. He was in town and wanted to see us. Great! I invited Helen — a mutual friend who hadn't seen Father in a long time — to come to our home, too.

Father Klyber arrived with a small package in his hand. He just loved marinated herring, and he had bought some on the way to our house. He nibbled, and we talked, while Florence cooked dinner.

During the meal, he exhibited some strange behavior. He jumped up several times, ran out of the room, came back, and gulped down a piece of bread. What was the matter with him?

After dinner he took me aside and quietly said, "I have a fish bone stuck in my throat."

I stared at him, "You have a *what?*"

"I have a fish bone in my throat."

I yelled, "For heaven's sake! Let's do something!"

I ran to find Florence's cousin John and asked him to drive Father to a hospital.

It was close to midnight when we returned to the house, minus the fish bone. Everyone was relieved — although worn out. Anxiety and the late hour had taken their toll.

We asked John to drive Father to the church where he was staying. It was St. Michael's on Cleveland Avenue, quite a distance from our house. On the way, he took Helen home.

☆ ☆ ☆

We arrived at the rectory. Father asked Florence and me inside for a moment, and there he began, "I wanted to talk to you all evening…" and he told us of a place that would just be ideal for us; we would feel perfectly at home there.

I wasn't interested. It sounded very familiar. Twice in the past he told me about a job that would be "just ideal" for me.

123

But I had a job; I had it for nine years. And Florence worked with me now. We had a good income, and I wasn't about to risk that for anything.

I looked at my watch. It was one o'clock in the morning. I had a cold and a slight fever and I was half-asleep. I only wanted to go home and go to bed.

I tried to end the conversation politely, so I asked, "Who runs this place?"

He snapped, "What do you mean, 'Who runs this place?' The priests of our Order!"

I awoke with a startled "Oh!...Ah...What do they do?"

"I told you what they do: They publish Catholic literature. You should see this place! It's a beehive of activity, and it runs with the precision of a Swiss watch. You would love it there! There you'd be working for God!"

We said a hurried good-bye, promising to talk again the next day. But the next day Father Klyber had changed his tune. He warned us against being overly enthusiastic, "Think about it calmly. It would mean moving your household to a different state and making new friends...."

The ruse didn't work; we were determined to see this place. When Saturday came, we boarded a train to St. Louis. The date was September 27, 1952. It happened to be my mother's birthday.

☆ ☆ ☆

Father Klyber met us at the station, put us into a car, and treated us to a visual feast. He drove into the country, through scenery of breathtaking beauty. Florence was exuberant. She had never seen anything like it in her life.

We arrived at The Place. It was a spot of unspoiled beauty, high up on a hill, studded with cedars, surrounded by other hills and small valleys. It bore a surprising resemblance to the Vienna woods where I had spent so many days of my life.

There were two large colonial-style mansions and some small cottages. I knew I could feel at home there.

Then we saw the "plant" which, in Father Klyber's words, was "a beehive of activity." (The "bees" were gone; it was Saturday.) All we saw was a large room in the center of one of the big, old buildings. It was cluttered with some mailing machines and stacks of magazines — nothing to suggest the "precision of a Swiss watch."

The next day we met the man in charge of the place. His name was Father Donald Miller. I said to him, "We always wanted to do something for God. Maybe this is our opportunity." It came from the heart.

He asked about our qualifications for the publishing business. We had none. He told us it would be some time before they could consider taking us; they were in the process of building. "But I'll show you the place where you would live." He took us to one of the cottages.

How can I describe it? In simple language: It was a shack. We entered through a porch which had no walls, only a roof held up by two wooden beams. There were three rooms. The one on the right was clean and orderly. An older man lived in it at the time, a retired nurse. The one on the left was a disaster area: a crumpled bed and clothes all over the floor. And the room in the middle? Picture an empty space with a gas heater and a long pipe going straight into the ceiling, and right next to it — out in the open — a hot-water heater with another long pipe going straight into the ceiling. Father Miller said, "We'd have to make it more livable before you'd come."

We said good-bye, and Father Klyber drove us back to the train. In the car he said, "You are very silent. Did the appearance of the house dampen your spirits?" The clown in me thought, "It didn't dampen them; it drowned them." But I kept silent. I wasn't in the mood for clowning. I had fallen in love with the place we had seen and with the idea of working for God.

Once on the train, Florence and I discussed what we could do to improve the appearance of the house. We suddenly realized that we hadn't even asked how much they would pay us. But it didn't matter. Everything paled in comparison to the privilege of being part of this important work. Our twenty-foot living room with its rose carpet now was just another room, and Sunnyside Avenue with its rows of elegant houses only another street.

We met Father Miller again at a friend's funeral in Chicago. Nothing was said about our possible move to Missouri. We waited. Then a letter came from Father Klyber. He said we should think carefully about moving to that place; in winter it was almost impossible to get out of it. But getting *out of it* was not our problem.

In March I decided to test the waters. I wrote to Father Miller and asked him if we had a chance. His reply filled us with a joy I cannot describe. He wrote, "I am convinced that divine Providence has a place for you in this apostolate."

A few weeks later we watched our furniture — piano, gas stove and all — being loaded onto a moving van, and we took, for the second and final time, the train to St. Louis. The date was May 1, 1953.

At the station, we were welcomed by three priests. They showed us the city, took us to dinner, and then to our new home. We found some changes. The "beehive" had left the cluttered mansion and moved into a brand-new modern building, completed only two weeks before we arrived.

But the greatest surprise was the little cottage; it had been transformed into a *home* — still plain, unadorned, waiting for our personal touch. But it was God's home for us, where we hoped to live *with* him and *for* him.

RICHER THAN
A MILLIONAIRE

I had wandered far and wide to come to this hour, seeking in creatures what only the Creator can give. And when I finally found him, with a heart full of gratitude, I eagerly tried to discover what I must do for him.

But he, in rare moments of solitude and silence, teaches me, not what I must *do* for him but what I must *be* for him.

He speaks, and my heart listens. My poor mind tries to follow the dictates of my heart. And if I'm too slow to grasp, I need not worry. He is there, with his endless patience.

He is my Father, my Friend, my Adonai, the faithful Companion who will never leave me until I reach my goal — until I come to the end of the journey.